MW01293191

Fred Rogers

A Captivating Guide to the Man Behind
Mister Rogers' Neighborhood

Free Bonus from Captivating History (Available for a Limited time)

Hi History Lovers!

Now you have a chance to join our exclusive history list so you can get your first history ebook for free as well as discounts and a potential to get more history books for free! Simply visit the link below to join.

Captivatinghistory.com/ebook

Also, make sure to follow us on Facebook, Twitter and Youtube by searching for Captivating History.

Contents

Introduction

There was no one quite like the man who talked kids through trips to the doctor and political assassinations all in the same careful, trustworthy tone of voice. With a patient, caring smile and a pretty little tune, this was a TV personality unlike any other at the time. Perhaps a bit old-fashioned and quaint to modern audiences, to the millions of children who watched him every day, he was engaging, friendly, and full of fun stories. That man, of course, was Mister Rogers, or Fred to his off-screen friends.

From 1968 to 2001, Mister Rogers was a staple of early childhood television. In lieu of fast-paced animated cartoons that pitted good guy against bad guy, Rogers' world of puppets, make-believe, and personal stories encouraged face-to-face connections between young children and the people around them. His domain, *Mister Rogers' Neighborhood*, included a wide world of characters, both puppet and human, created by Rogers and often voiced by the man himself. It was a world of imagination and play, but Mister Rogers also encouraged his viewers to discern between make-believe and reality. He showed them factories and public spaces and explained how parts of the real world worked through video segments in each episode, sometimes tackling controversial issues such as physical disabilities, mental health, war, and death.

Mister Rogers was more than just a puppeteer, a teacher, or an entertainer, though he was all those things; he was also a trusted friend and advisor. Rogers spoke personably with kids and helped them identify and organize their emotions. He explained how to deal with anger in simple, relatable terms and sang songs to help his guests and viewers cope with their feelings. He told generations of young people that it was okay to cry and show emotion since these are feelings every person experiences.

Said the man himself:

> Confronting our feelings and giving them appropriate expression always takes strength, not weakness. It takes strength to acknowledge our anger, and sometimes more strength yet to curb the aggressive urges anger may bring and to channel them into nonviolent outlets.

No matter the topic of discussion, Mister Rogers always greeted his audience with a smile and a tune.

He sang, "Would you be mine, could you be mine, won't you be my neighbor?"

Would that they could have been!

This is the story of everyone's favorite neighbor.

Chapter One – A Boy with a Name That Said It All

On March 20th, 1928, James and Nancy Rogers of Latrobe, Pennsylvania welcomed a new son into their well-to-do family. It was from Nancy's father that her newborn son got his name: the wonderfully apt Fred McFeely Rogers. The little boy lived up to his name almost immediately, showing great affection for his family and inanimate toys. An only child for most of his youth, Fred learned to keep himself entertained with hand-made puppets, books, music, and his very own imagination.

Sadly for young Fred, the future beloved children's television host was also quite sensitive to a variety of illnesses. Burdened with breathing difficulties, seasonal allergies, and various childhood illnesses, little Fred McFeely Rogers often found himself sick at home instead of learning at school—and this part of his life almost certainly played a large part in the development of his famous personality.

Suffering frequently from asthma that kept him out of school, young Fred learned to keep good company within the family unit, and he was no stranger to the loving administrations of his parents and maternal grandfather Fred McFeely. The two shared a special bond and the elder Fred—owner of the very successful McFeely Brick— taught his grandson to play the piano. Fred was a very eager and talented student. The original Mr. McFeely was an excellent pianist, and he spent countless hours showing his young grandson how to play a tune. In many interviews later in life, Rogers described the closest of ties between his maternal grandfather and himself. The piano became a wonderful and expressive tool for young Fred, who would play with his grandfather and then hand the instrument over to his mother to play so he could sing along. It was at the piano with Mr. McFeely that his love of music and composition was born and nurtured.

At the feet of his gentle family, Rogers learned at a young age how to deal with his feelings and emotions in ways that were productive. The Rogers were a quite well-to-do family thanks to the solid businesses owned by both Fred's grandfathers, and they regularly attended church. The family took their Christian teachings seriously, making efforts to volunteer, give to charity, and generally have a caring attitude. Nancy even wanted to become a doctor but instead was a lifelong volunteer at the local hospital. This attitude helped shape Fred's belief in the importance of teaching emotional maturity, particularly in a world where incidents of violence seemed to always be on the rise. In the epic four-hour interview for the Archive of American Television, he said, "There are many ways in which you can express yourself without hurting anybody."

When Fred's paternal grandfather died, his father grieved openly in front of the family. It was another important, character-building moment in the boy's life. "I remember after my grandfather's death, seeing Dad in the hall with tears streaming down his face. I don't think I had ever seen him cry before. I'm glad I did see him. It helped me know that it was okay for men to cry." This was a time in the USA when old-fashioned values kept emotions in check behind a stiff upper lip as men needed to be seen as strong; for Fred to have witnessed how to deal with grief at a young age, it must have had quite an effect on his mind and helped to shape him into the compassionate Mister Rogers the world came to love.

At a later point in his life, while comforting someone whose grandfather had died, Mister Rogers shared a story about his own grandfather, saying that he had given him an old boat which they worked on together. There would come a time when he would have neither his grandfather nor his boat, but he did have the work ethic that his grandfather had instilled in him while working on the boat together.

Rogers himself described his family as warm and caring. They created a home where he knew he was loved and where that love could be shared with a newcomer, Fred's adopted sister Elaine. Fred was already 11 years old when his sister came to live with the Rogers family, but the siblings shared their space happily and became very close. In later years, Fred would name one of his famous *Neighborhood* characters after Elaine.

Though he was showered with kindness from a loving family at home, he was exposed to the colder sides of life when he was out in the world by himself as a younger boy. Reportedly overweight and often ill, young Fred Rogers was a victim of schoolyard bullying. In later years, Rogers told interviewers that he was walking home from school one day when other kids started taunting him about his body shape. He was an introverted child by some accounts, so he was sooner found with a book than on a playing field. On top of that, add months of every year where he was bedridden by an illness. The kids called him fat, and he made for home, perhaps more than once, to his family for comfort, stung by the nastiness of others. Perhaps this is where he learned his first lesson on the importance of kindness, by feeling the unkindness or cruelty of others.

Throughout Fred's youth, the actions of his peers left him feeling downcast and unappreciated. Thanks to the unwavering support and genuine compassion of his family, he fortunately found stability and love. Though school had been tough for Fred as a young boy, he found a more welcoming environment once he reached high school and made several friends.

As tough as life was sometimes, young Fred Rogers didn't lose his love for his home, family, or his world of make-believe. He always knew that he was coming home to a family who treasured him, and that was so much more important than the bad things that happened in the outside world. Perhaps, in later years, it was Fred's familial stability that gave him the confidence to put himself on a public platform, even if that surely meant facing criticism. In so many ways, Fred's parents, grandparents, and sister were responsible for turning this boy into a respectful, gentle, and intelligent man with the courage to stand up for what he believed in.

Though stardom was definitely not something he had in mind, Fred had an open path before him which would eventually—and somewhat ironically—be graced with a Hollywood Star.

Chapter Two – The College Years

When Fred graduated from Latrobe High School in 1946 and started college, the world around him was shifting. A cultural revolution was putting down roots and preparing to radically change the status quo in America. In print, on radio waves, and soon by television, the equality movement was on the march, and young Fred was very much aware of it when he made the move from high school to college. In his young adulthood, television increasingly became the most captivating form of entertainment and news, and the industry's rapid growth alongside modern feminism and equal rights activism had a big impact on the young man.

At the same time, television was starting its own revolution in news and entertainment. At a time when Fred was seriously contemplating his future career, he marveled at how negatively the influx of advertisements affected such a promising new technology. He began to sincerely hate television programming, yet he was captivated by it all the same. What Rogers saw on TV—which was at the time comprised of mostly news, game shows, cowboy stories, and musical variety hours—was often disappointing to him. Despite the advertisements and violence, Rogers still saw the medium for what it had to offer. He knew that television could be a force for good, if only it were operated by the right people.

With high school over, Rogers struggled to make up his mind about what to study at college. He strongly considered going to seminary school but also was very interested in musical composition and, of course, television. Accepted to Dartmouth College, his first studies focused on diplomacy but were quickly switched when the young student had an epiphany: he most definitely wanted to study music instead. While talking to the head of his department at Dartmouth about his interest in switching majors, he discovered that there was not yet a full music program at his current school. The head of his department suggested he go to Rollins College in Florida, which was well-known for its music department.

Fred decided to travel to Rollins College during Easter break to see what their music department had to offer. On arriving in Florida, the distinction between the two schools was immediately clear to him— not the least of which was Rollins' warm climate. And it wasn't just the weather that was warm, for he also received an earnest welcome from his future fellow students. He didn't need much more convincing even though he would need to do an extra year of work at Rollins to compensate for the switch; Rogers made the switch and didn't look back.

Making the switch to Rollins College didn't just change Rogers' future career and legacy, but it also led him to a person who would become one of the most important in his life: Sara Joanne Byrd. A fellow college student, Joanne—which she preferred to be called— immediately captured Fred's attention. Joanne was also a musician who specialized in playing and composing for the piano, earning a bachelor's in music from Rollins. When she graduated from Rollins, she moved onto Florida State University to study under the renown Hungarian composer, Ernst von Dohnanyi.

Fred and Joanne also had a tight group of friends at school, and together they had an unforgettable time while honing their skills as musicians. In later years, when writing the introduction to *The World According to Mister Rogers*, Joanne described Fred as a kind and compassionate person, even in his early adulthood. Though he was quite social at college, Fred chose neither to drink alcohol or smoke tobacco. Though the pair's close relationship probably led others at school to consider them sweethearts, Fred and Joanne spent their college years as friends and nothing more.

Always a good student, Fred excelled at his music studies. As everyone enrolled at the college was expected to take a variety of classes, some outside their major, Fred wound up learning a little bit of French. For practice using the language, Rogers' teacher asked him to put on small theatrical pieces that were scripted in French. As much as the little productions might seem like a glimpse into Rogers' future work, he didn't actually feel very comfortable performing in front of people. These experiences made him yearn for a creative spot just a little closer to the shadows than to center stage.

Unlike Joanne, who attended Rollins to perfect her piano playing, Fred decided to focus on composition as a way to combine his musical interests with the television industry. As new networks formed and started to produce a variety of musical programs, there was a serious need for staff who actually knew how to put music together and deal with musical equipment. Ironically, the Rogers' family didn't even have a television set in their home—Fred's parents actually found his intentions to work in TV a little baffling. They couldn't argue about his employment prospects, however, since the industry was clearly booming.

After a total of five years in college—Dartmouth and Rollins combined—Fred graduated with a degree in musical composition in 1951. After leaving campus, Rogers went eight months without seeing Joanne before he wrote her a letter proposing marriage. She accepted, and they married on June 9th, 1952.

Chapter Three – Family Life

As Fred Rogers himself wrote in *The World According to Mister Rogers*, "To love someone is to strive to accept that person exactly the way he or she is, right here and now." As a very faithful Christian man, Fred believed in working to make a marriage last. Fortunately, he had found himself the perfect partner in Joanne, and the couple's friendship endured all the normal hardships through which a married pair can suffer. Though Joanne didn't know about Fred's fascination with children and children's education until they were married, she was more than happy to indulge his wishes for the family.

When Fred had proposed to Joanne, it was from his new home in New York City, where he had secured a job in television. After their marriage in 1952, she joined him there. The couple soon had two sons together, James and John. Every bit as calm and calculating as he was with his television viewers later on, Fred was a devoted and loving father. He was slow to punish the boys for their minor misbehavior, which left much of the active disciplining to his wife. That said, Fred often used the voice of Lady Elaine Fairchilde around the house, which in the Neighborhood of Make-Believe was the closest thing there was to a nagging parent.

In later years, the boys struggled to carry the weight of their seemingly perfect television dad, often being teased at school. The boys sometimes found it difficult to cope with the fact that everyone around them—their peers, teachers, and, of course, their neighbors—knew their father as Mister Rogers. Coping as best they could, both boys were integrated into the television show that meant so much to their father. In fact, both boys visited their father on set several times during their childhood, starting with the very first season of *Mister Rogers' Neighborhood* on American public television. It was 1968 when a young Jamie Rogers came to the set to play with his dad, bringing some children's clay with him. The two shaped it into a baseball diamond. In Episode 66 that same year, John came by to play with some toy cars and sit with his dad in a rocking chair while Fred sang "Please Don't Think It's Funny."

Rogers' sons would continually appear on the set into the mid-1970s, but they stopped visiting the on-camera Neighborhood when they were in their later teens. In the 2018 documentary, "Won't You Be My Neighbor?" John admitted that "It was a little tough having the second Christ as my dad." As for James, usually called Jamie, it was even tougher. His teen years were tumultuous, and when he was at Rollins College in 1978, *People* magazine published an article in which both Fred and Joanne admitted Jamie was no longer speaking to his family.

"It's been painful," said Fred, "and it's rough on Jamie [James], but if we don't allow him to go off and have this time for himself, he'll never come back to the nest." Forty years later, Jim told documentary filmmakers that he wasn't too pleased with that particular article. Once he had struck out on his own, however, things between himself and his parents gradually warmed back up. Fred made an effort to accept his son as a different sort of person and young man than he had been, which helped ease the tension in their relationship. "Dad always gave me room to grow. I've had a beard and long hair for a pretty long time, and he always thought of that as outside stuff that didn't really matter. I can remember him saying one time he wished he could grow a beard so that people wouldn't recognize him."

In Episode 1623 of *Mister Rogers' Neighborhood,* which aired originally in 1990, a particularly jovial Fred talked about "Fathers and Music" and welcomed his own son Jim, fully-grown and sporting a thick mustache. Jim had an extra little person with him as well—Fred's grandson Alexander. The three of them sat down at the piano, and Fred reminded his son of a song they used to play with John. Together, they played a happy little tune before showing Alexander the trolley and playing a game of peek-a-boo. When the visitors departed, Rogers sang "It's Such a Good Feeling" before quickly trotting off to join his family members out in the real world.

Chapter Four – Working for NBC

"I got into television because I hated it so, and I thought there's some way of using this fabulous instrument to nurture those who would watch and listen." Rogers was right; there was still space for television to develop in another direction, and he was just the person to start the transition.

Fred applied for a job with NBC immediately upon graduating from Rollins College and was accepted. He went straight from Winter Park, Florida to New York City and got to work in 1951, hoping to change the face of television by working within the industry. Having easily obtained the position thanks to his degree in musical composition, Fred was hired to work on various NBC musical programs. It was exactly what he had planned and hoped for, but it was ultimately a letdown. It seemed that even from the inside of the studio, television just wasn't living up to Fred's exacting standards. Helping to produce a number of NBC shows was, however, an integral part of his vocational training.

As assistant producer and network floor director on several shows, Rogers discovered that it would be much more difficult to change TV than he had originally hoped. Whereas he imagined that television productions could be both entertaining and educational, there was little of the latter to offer, particularly for kids. Shows like *Dennis the Menace*, *The Mickey Mouse Club*, *The Adventures of Rin Tin Tin*, and *Lassie* were popular; however, they were studded with advertisements and not particularly focused on the mental and emotional development of very young viewers.

During his time with the NBC network, Rogers worked on *The Gabby Hayes Show*, *Your Hit Parade*, *The Kate Smith Hour*, and *The Voice of Firestone*. In all, he ended up spending only a year in New York City, and though it gave him a priceless experience in the television industry, he did not particularly enjoy his time with the company. In all of these positions, however, he was utilizing the music skills he learned as part of his degree in music while learning how shows operated and the floors were managed.

Most of the shows Rogers helped produce were musicals, from *The Hit Parade*'s top tracks to Kate Smith's Christian songs and *The Voice of Firestone*'s classical orchestra. Acting as floor manager for *The Gabby Hayes Show* was probably the most inspirational of Rogers' work with NBC as it was produced for children. Hayes was a movie star best known for his roles in westerns like *The Cariboo Trail* and *The Nevada Buckaroo*, but in his later years, he switched media and became a television personality. Hayes presented clips from cowboy movies and told stories, as well as promoting the show's sponsor, Quaker Oats, by firing the cereal grains from a cannon. For Rogers, who was not a fan of guns and violence in children's entertainment, it may have been a bit conflicting to help present such segments to young viewers.

Nevertheless, Rogers had a young family to support, and it wouldn't look good to other potential employers if he ditched his first industry job right away. So, he persevered and learned all he could, especially from Hayes. Intrigued by the man's ability to step in front of a television camera so confidently, Fred asked Hayes how he managed to be on camera knowing so many people were watching. Hayes told Rogers that it was all about talking to just "one little buckaroo"—in other words, the key was to focus on just one person and chat with them as if you were one-on-one.

With some of his time off, Fred explored the city and found himself regularly volunteering at children's homes, orphanages, and daycares where he could interact with children. Never before having considered a career working with kids, Rogers found with some surprise that he was starting to lean in that direction. His volunteer work and his professional work on *The Gabby Hayes Show* revealed an innate need in the young man to provide educational sustenance for the young children of the world. Working on Hayes' and other NBC shows convinced Rogers that quality children's entertainment couldn't be properly produced with so much interruption and reliance on commercial sponsors.

While learning just what it took to get a television show taped and ran on-air, another part of Rogers' mind was busy considering other options. So, as he worked as a floor manager, making sure that the equipment was set up properly, that actors and guests were in the right place, and checking the timings and dealing with minute-by-minute issues, he watched the various shows he was a part of unfold and considered how he might do things differently were he in charge.

For three years, he worked hard and was given more and more responsibility at the NBC station, and as a highly-valued member of the team, he was on a career track to become a well-paid producer. However, Fred knew that he needed to work on something more fulfilling. When he decided that it was finally time to step away from the network and move back to Pennsylvania with his family, Rogers' first priority was to find another job in television—this time without commercials and in a position where he could call the shots. In 1954, the right opportunity came along at WQED Pittsburgh, just a short drive from where Fred had grown up in Latrobe. The station had contacted him in November of the previous year, asking if he'd like to be a part of a team putting together a brand-new public access channel. The short answer was "yes."

Chapter Five – Public Television and The Children's Corner

After leaving his floor manager position with NBC, the next important step in Fred's career was centered around a WQED show called *The Children's Corner*. It was an hour-long show, and initially, his job was to be the organist and composer. As Rogers preferred, the position was mostly behind the scenes, where he was able to freely develop characters and a unique style of musical composition aimed at kids. The behind-the-scenes aspect of television production was suited to his somewhat shy demeanor, but unlike at NBC, Fred was an important part of creating the show's actual content.

WQED was a unique channel. It created educational content and was considered America's first community-sponsored show, with *The Children's Corner* later becoming an award-winning program. Fred was an integral part of that success, but even so, he never imagined himself taking a position in front of the camera, nor did he think that his childhood love of puppets would eventually work its way into his professional life—but of course, he was wrong on both counts. The magical moment that put Fred Rogers on television was due to a piece of brittle film that broke during WQED's first broadcast.

"Well, I didn't realize it, but those films were very brittle at times. And, of course, everything was live. And we'd be on the air. And here would be a film showing, and it would break. We'd have to fill with something. And so the night before we went on the air, Mrs. Dorothy Daniel, who was the general manager of the station, gave me a little tiger puppet. So I called him Daniel for her. And when the first film broke, I just poked the puppet through. And this was just a very fanciful set with drawings on it. And I just poked him through, and it happened to be a clock where I poked him through. And he just said, it's 5:02, and Columbus discovered America in 1492. And that was the first thing that I ever said through puppetry on the air."

The Children's Corner was hosted by a young woman named Josie Carey, who was a very talented musician, composer, and singer. She welcomed her young audience members to Calendarland, where various creatures lived and shared their stories. The program was largely musical, which was where Fred came in to help her write and play the songs. After his little stint with Daniel Tiger, however, he was convinced to try his hand—literally—at some of the show's puppetry. Very soon, he was the voice and movement behind a small cast of puppet characters who would stay with him for a lifetime.

In the guise of Daniel Tiger, Grandpere, Henrietta Pussycat, and X the Owl, Fred had reluctantly made it onto the small screen. Together, Josie and Fred composed dozens of popular children's songs that were released on vinyl records for Pittsburgh fans. They also wrote a book together, *Our Small World*, that featured all their puppet characters, including King Friday and an early version of Lady Elaine. Within the book was a two-page illustration of the layout of Calendarland, including Daniel Tiger's clock, King Friday's castle, and the Eiffel Tower. The book was published with 5,000 copies being sold around the Pittsburgh area.

In time, Fred himself—looking dapper in a jacket and bow tie with coiffed hair—appeared on camera in minor roles. He was learning to become a little more comfortable on the other side of the camera, which made it easier for him to participate in the creative process with his co-composer, the producer, and stage managers. It was a formative role for the young Rogers, who would use many of the puppets, characters, and show formats within *The Children's Corner* for his own productions later in his career. The show lasted from 1954 to 1961, during which time Fred and Josie wrote 68 songs together. When it was over, Josie was offered several roles with other networks creating children's programming. She continued to do so until the mid-1990s.

Before *The Children's Corner* finished, however, Rogers proved a wonderful addition to the cast and production crew. It was very important work in Fred's mind, but it wasn't just the show that occupied his mind at that point in time. He was a father, a husband, and also a man in search of deeper spiritual knowledge. Fred Rogers loved his work on television and was growing to love it more with the potential he saw in supporting children socially and emotionally. What he did not love was the glitz and glamor, the smoke and mirrors that drew most people into what advertising wanted TV to seem like.

Similar to his student days, as an adult, Fred Rogers never smoked nor drank. His time outside of work was not spent in bars, gentlemen's clubs, or in rehabilitation centers, unlike many of his television peers. Instead, while working at WQED, on his lunch breaks Fred took a short walk every day to take part in something that one might suggest guided his television work: He was studying to be a Presbyterian minister at the Pittsburgh Theological Seminary.

Though he had already completed his music degree and made strides within the television industry, Rogers didn't feel that his personal education was complete. He had been raised by devout Christian parents who practiced advocacy, generosity, and compassion. His mother and father were highly respected in Latrobe, and they imparted a sense of community responsibility and pride in their children. Nancy McFeely Rogers had plans to become a doctor, but when she found she hadn't the time to devote herself to medical school, she settled for spending her free time volunteering in the local hospital.

His upbringing instilled within him a deep connection with Christianity, and therefore, in the early 1960s, Fred joined the Pittsburgh Theological Seminary as a student. Having found life outside Pennsylvania not particularly to his liking, Rogers probably took great comfort in attending a seminary school so close to his hometown and family. The school, built at the end of the 18th century not long after the city itself was founded, focused on preparing students for a future as clergy members of the Presbyterian faith. As the school's own rhetoric says, students are taught to minister "in the way of Jesus."

The Presbyterian Church in the USA shares its roots in the Protestant Reformation of the European Renaissance, specifically in terms of Calvinism. Its constituents separated from the Catholic Church on many premises, primarily whether individuals could own and read the Bible. Believing in the ability of the average person to interpret the gospels of their own accord, Protestant religions such as the Presbyterian Church undertook a largely progressive path. It was these humanist-derived teachings that were imparted on Fred, both as the child of Presbyterian parents and as an adult student.

Rogers' theology education included such courses as rural ministry, the history of Israel, religion and ecology, Hebrew grammar, and evangelism. At the end of his studies in 1963, 35-year-old Fred Rogers graduated as an ordained minister of the United Presbyterian Church. Upon graduation, Rogers told interviewers later that his seminary advisors told him that the best way he could serve the church was to continue creating and presenting children's television entertainment. It was a piece of advice that Rogers was entirely happy to follow, though he very rarely mentioned religion on camera. The only exception to this general rule was during national mourning or emergency episodes of *Mister Rogers' Neighborhood*.

Despite rarely using the word "God" or "church" in his various books and television shows, Rogers nevertheless always behaved as his religious beliefs compelled him. He was a staunch advocate for youth and the disabled; he spoke about understanding one's feelings to control personal anger, and he was a strong example of kind parenting and loving fatherhood.

Chapter Six – Misterogers and the Canadian Broadcasting Corporation

Contrary to the belief of most Mister Rogers' fans, the iconic show didn't first air on PBS. Before the legendary *Mister Rogers' Neighborhood* was fully conceived, Fred was offered the chance to work on an early incarnation of the show north of the border. It was in the early 1960s that Fred Rogers and his young family moved to Toronto, Canada, where he had been offered a position by the Canadian Broadcasting Corporation (CBC). It was an opportunity to produce and work on his own children's music show—a chance he couldn't turn down.

Before the move was even on the table, Rogers was fresh out of seminary school and happily acting on the advice of his teachers— seeking out opportunities to promote the Christian faith on television. He quickly joined up with a group of producers from the church who were in the midst of planning a children's television series from the pulpit, and he excitedly started to organize the logistics of the program. The day before the show was meant to go into production, however, it was called off due to a lack of sufficient funding.

Rogers must have been considerably worried, having no other job prospects lined up, but it turned out he only went one day without an offer. The very next day after the church project fell apart, CBC got in touch and asked him to join their team. Excited and relieved, Fred agreed immediately—even though taking the job meant emigrating. Without another option, the Rogers did their best to embrace the move.

Moving to Toronto was not what Fred, Joanne, and their sons John and James expected to do at that point in their lives, mainly because the whole family—Fred included—believed that Fred would take a position with the Pittsburgh church. Nevertheless, as strong as his faith was in the Presbyterian Church, Fred's future was not based within the walls of a place of worship, and he knew it. Television was what he had wanted to work in since going to college, and so he'd actively seek out positions with local and international channels.

The move to Canada was significant not only because it marked such a big move and Fred's first role at the helm of children's programming, but because he would no longer be behind the scenes of the show. Personally, Fred had ideally imagined a refreshing and relatively slow-moving show that involved his own music and puppetry, but a role as host of the show never crossed his mind. As it happened, however, CBC wanted to put Fred Rogers in front of the camera, not behind it.

Said the man himself, "I never expected to be on the screen, ever. I expected that I could work with children one-to-one, but I don't think that I ever expected to be on the television."

Fortunately for Mister Rogers' fans, the producer of the show said that all he wanted Fred to do was be himself. That producer's name was Fred Rainsbury, and he wanted Rogers to write the music for the show as well as personally interact with children who visited the set. As Rogers' personality and plots were to be the subject of the show, it was simply named *Misterogers*.

Each CBC episode was fifteen minutes long and featured several of Rogers' own character creations for whom he also provided the voices. Many of his puppets had come from *The Children's Corner* and would later feature in Rogers' long-lived PBS show. One of those characters was the hand puppet, Daniel S. Tiger, straight out of *The Children's Corner* studio. Manipulated and voiced by Rogers, Daniel Tiger was a big hit with kids—and they didn't seem to care that Mister Rogers was no ventriloquist. Fred clearly had his arm behind the tiger when Daniel moved and moved his lips when the tiger spoke. It didn't matter; the audience had plenty of imagination, just like their host.

Already, Fred's trademark look had begun to appear—sneakers and a hand-knitted cardigan sweater from his mother, complete with a zipper up the front. She made him a new one every year. Rogers' previous television work had convinced him that formal work shoes had no place on a sound stage, so he naturally formed the habit of switching into softer-soled shoes once he had taken his place in front of the camera. It was a move that stuck and would be satirized by comedians for decades to come.

Rogers remembered the advice he had been given from Gabby Hayes about presenting a show, so when he accepted the *Misterogers* show and stepped in front of the camera lens, that's what he focused on. Fred consistently concentrated on reaching one child at a time, believing that if he could connect to that one person watching, the production was worthwhile. In doing so, Rogers transferred his own calm, likable persona onto the screen, justifying Rainsbury in his choice of host. According to Rogers, television was a special way to communicate with the whole world, because when you see someone speaking directly into the camera, it feels as if they are speaking directly to you.

As *Misterogers* grew in popularity, Fred Rogers learned how to comfortably compose himself on camera and portray the lovable, trustworthy host so many of us remember. Working with the CBC team and Ernie Coombs—an assistant puppeteer from Maine who'd previously worked with Fred on *The Children's Corner*—Rogers created enough 15-minute episodes of *Misterogers* to keep the show going for four seasons. After a three-year stint in Canada, however, Fred and his wife decided they ultimately wanted to raise their sons back in Pennsylvania. They parted ways with CBC, packed up their belongings, and trekked back down into the United States in 1964, armed with a solid children's program premise and several puppet characters. The network allowed Rogers to take the characters he had created but kept its own copyright on the episodes they'd produced with him.

It's interesting to note that Fred's assistant puppeteer, Ernie Coombs, decided to stay in Canada. He put together the hit CBC children's show *Mr. Dressup*, which he hosted in very much the same style as Rogers, complete with puppets and a make-believe realm in which Coombs wore costumes he procured from his famous Tickle Trunk. *Mr. Dressup* ran for over 30 years and is a beloved part of childhood for several generations of Canadians.

As for Rogers, he had learned just about everything he needed to put together the same show back in America, where it would change children's entertainment forever.

Chapter Seven – Mister Rogers' Neighborhood

When Joanne Rogers describes her husband in the prologue to *The World According to Mister Rogers*, she notes that there was "a sense of hard-work and inner discipline to his work." She went on to describe what others may call perfectionism, as he was determined to do the very best he could. Since his on-screen persona is so calm and well-polished, it would be easy to assume his writing process went just as smoothly as a recording session. On the contrary, "he fretted over the words, attempting to make the content meaningful."

Desiring the Canadian episodes for his own use, Fred set about obtaining the rights to his CBC show. This did not happen overnight, but all of the elements of his past came together when he created a more complete educational program that once more took his name and in which he created a global, televised community.

When he first returned from Toronto, Fred didn't have a show or network to return to, although he did have a job from the church to fall back on. However, shortly after his return, a friend who owned a store asked for some Christmas shows in the lead-up to Christmas using puppets, which got Rogers back into filming. Once the commercials were filmed using the puppets, Fred assembled a team, rented buildings, spaces, and equipment, and made 100 shows that were each about fifteen minutes in length. It was a successful project with one exception: Rogers had unknowingly vetoed his right to redistribute the shows. Though he would have liked to add them to his collection along with the CBC episodes he won the rights to in 1966, he rarely uses these episodes or their music today. As he put it, "Why pay to use them when we can write new ones?"

Fortunately for Fred and his family, job offers were never few or far between for the musician, producer, and puppeteer. This time, it was the Eastern Educational Network, another publicly funded television channel, that wanted to work with him. Rogers signed on to put together some brand-new episodes of his show, this time under the title *Mister Rogers' Neighborhood.* He spent his time developing his new show, built on his history of work and his degree in music composition. Many of the later famous set pieces from *Mister Rogers' Neighborhood,* such as Trolley and the Eiffel Tower, first appeared on the CBC show of the nearly-identical name.

Thanks to his studies at seminary school, Fred Rogers may well be the only ordained minister in the world who put his family-counseling training to work through mass media. The church was still happy for him to teach and work with kids, so that's what Fred did. He taught not only the kids watching the shows but their parents too. It was about nurturing and learning, taught in a loving, musical, story-filled way.

Finally, the epitome of Rogers' television experience—as far as his intergenerational audience members are concerned—had come to fruition. Using set pieces from the CBC, musical experience from *The Children's Corner,* floor management skills and techniques from NBC, and presentation advice from Gabby Hayes, Fred Rogers morphed into his not-so-alter-ego, Mister Rogers. Using the opening and closing of the show from Canada, they included and expanded the Neighborhood of Make-Believe, and made more puppets. One hour of production was needed for every minute of the show, simple as the format may seem. Since each episode was roughly half an hour in length, that represented 30 hours of studio work and about $6,000.

Mister Rogers' Neighborhood had a live band and always followed the same routine when the host entered his on-set house. He started to slowly sing his intro theme, "Won't you be my neighbor?" while taking off his jacket and switching it for a cardigan that was waiting for him in the closet near the door. Then he'd sit down, take off his shoes, and replace them with sneakers, smiling broadly or gently, depending on how he felt that day—a crucial element of the realism in everyone's lives—at the camera.

Each episode of *Mister Rogers' Neighborhood* was split into three main segments: An introductory piece in Rogers' home, an educational visit to an off-set location like a crayon factory, and a trip to the puppet-inhabited Neighborhood of Make-Believe. The latter was such an exclusive area that not even Mister Rogers could go there—only the audience and Trolley, a magical miniature railcar that made regular stops in Fred's living room, were allowed to go there. When it was time to visit the land of imagination, the eye of the camera followed Trolley through a dark tunnel built into the back of a window seat. The magical railcar soon emerged on an elevated track encircling a miniature castle, which is when the audience knew they had arrived in The Neighborhood of Make-Believe.

The action there usually started at King Friday's Castle, where a benevolent—if not a bit self-involved and scatterbrained—puppet king ruled over the people of Make-Believe. King Friday XIII often planned large parties, contests, and events for the kingdom but needed a lot of help from other citizens to get those plans off the ground. King Friday was a lifelong music lover who played the bass violin and eventually founded the King Friday Queen Sara Saturday Royal Foundation for the Performing Arts (KFQSSRFFTPA) with his royal wife.

The kingdom of Friday XIII didn't end at the castle borders. Very much like Calendarland had been on *The Children's Corner*, the Neighborhood of Make-Believe stretched for imaginary miles to encompass the various homes and workplaces of the puppets and humans who called it home. To the left of the castle was the Eiffel Tower, painted red, blue, and green. The Tower was home to Grandpere Tiger. Farther out was the Frog Pond, soon to be replaced by the Platypus Mound when the Frogg family moved house. Other structures included the Tele-can (a can-and-string used like a telephone), the Rocking Chair Factory, the Grandfather Clock where Daniel S. Tiger lived (just as he had since turning up unannounced one day on WQED when the film snapped), and Henrietta Pussycat's Great Oak Tree was in the center of the community.

The Museum-Go-Round, a circular building with multiple pillars and a bell, was home to Lady Elaine Fairchilde—an ugly and rather blunt character whose namesake was Rogers' own adopted sister. The puppet may not have been classically beautiful, but there was no love lost between Fred and the real Elaine. In fact, Lady Elaine represented a voice of reason and logic in the Neighborhood. Lady Elaine's museum home was seemingly endless inside, with countless rooms and treasures hidden within its walls—including a collection of trolleys that are all different from the one that travels between Mister Rogers' house and the Neighborhood of Make-Believe. The puppets discover this fact in Episode 1666 when the original red Trolley goes missing.

The most commonly seen characters of the Neighborhood of Make-Believe were Lady Elaine Fairchilde, Daniel S. Tiger, Henrietta Pussycat, X the Owl, and the human characters known as Lady Aberlin, Mr. McFeely, Officer Clemmons, and Chef Brockett. Mr. McFeely, the Speedy Delivery man, was named in honor of Fred's own grandfather, the same one who taught him to play the piano. Sometimes, the characters in the Neighborhood of Make-Believe interacted with characters from nearby realms, such as Someplace Else, the Cities of Westwood and Southwood, the Area of Northwood, and the Land of Allmine. Even farther out was the Planet Purple. On Planet Purple, all the boys and girls were purple, identical, and named either "Paul" or "Pauline." The only other residents are Purple Panda and Little Panda.

In the documentary, *Won't You Be My Neighbor?*, his wife said that there was a little bit of Fred in every puppet. When he was younger, he was more like the sweet and curious Daniel, but as time progressed, he became more like the benevolent monarch, King Friday XIII. Throughout the series, Fred always loved and enjoyed whimsical play.

Not only was *Mister Rogers' Neighborhood* a show with music and puppets, but it also had friends come to visit, as well as trips out in the world to see where things got made in factories. There was one trip, for instance, to see how balloons are made. Mister Roger didn't glorify one type of job over another; he just marveled at how the workers did their jobs and asked the workers questions about it.

During four special episodes, Joanne Rogers appeared on the program. In Episode 1439, she meets up with her husband at the end of the show when it is time for them to attend her piano recital. In the next episode, Mister Rogers shows a clip of his wife's recital to viewers. Altogether, Joanne and their sons appear on the show 17 times.

Chapter Eight – Program Themes and Distribution

Mister Rogers' Neighborhood was first distributed and televised in 1968 in black and white. It was picked up by a few educational channels in New York, Washington, D.C, and Boston. A move to the Public Broadcasting Service (PBS) in 1970 is what really took *Mister Rogers' Neighborhood* to every household in America. By that stage, it had been nearly twenty years since Fred Rogers entered the world of television as a fresh graduate with a different way of looking at the medium.

His work was always about presenting challenging topics wrapped in kindness and compassion, letting viewers see in practice what it meant to be a good neighbor. Fred Rogers was not out to convert the masses to his way of believing. Instead, he took the values of his religious belief system and embodied them in the characters within a format for a show designed for the most impressionable people on the planet. The kindness and caring, as well as the security and routine, he showed could also have served to help teach parents, many of whom might not have been taught with kindness themselves.

As for the CBC episodes Rogers had gained access to in 1966, these he put on-air via his old network, WQED. He also went back to work there himself, though not in the same capacity as before. This time, he rented his own studio and office space within the WQED buildings so his team could produce *Mister Rogers' Neighborhood* privately and therefore retain all copyrights without question. It was a bold move inspired by a strange incident one day in Fred Rogers' very own home.

One morning in 1970, Fred went to his front door to collect his daily carton of milk. When he reached down to get his carton, he saw his own face looking back at him. It was an advertisement. Nobody at the station had asked for his permission, and Rogers was no more agreeable to commercials than he had been in the 1950s. Aside from the commercial he had produced with a puppet after returning from Canada, Fred had never participated in advertising, nor did he want to—especially with his own face as the subject matter.

The realization that he wasn't in complete control of his image or work at his current studio taught Rogers that he needed to start handling the business end of *Neighborhood* as well as the creative end. For this reason, Family Communications, Inc. was born in 1971. A registered non-profit organization, Rogers believed Family Communications would be a better steward of the funds received by *Mister Rogers' Neighborhood* than other financial institutions available to him. So, instead of being employees of WQED, Rogers and his *Neighborhood* team became tenants.

They rented studios and equipment from WQED and moved in. The only change to the show was that all copyright moved to the non-profit organization. Relieved at his own innovative solution, Rogers went back to filming and rejected the idea that his show should be capitalized with themed memorabilia put on sale. Despite being targeted to children and childhood themes, his shows weren't meant to bring in sales and make Fred a millionaire. His episodes were radical in their own way at the time, not only because of their lack of commercialization but in pertinent content.

His message was never overtly religious; instead, it was the embodiment of the values of his faith and belief system. He tackled divorce, death, and other real-life topics like making friends, the first day of school, and how to deal with your feelings. The message was a positive one, even if the darker side of life needed to be discussed for a few minutes. The idea behind *Neighborhood* was that community could give you the strength to continue if you didn't feel you had it yourself.

Spanning the late 1960s to the early 2000s, *Mister Rogers Neighborhood* continued to gently support social diversity in a crucial time period. Sticking hard to his message that every child is special, Rogers welcomed not only the black Officer Clemmons to his show, but he enjoyed an on-screen visit from an interracial group of students and their black teacher, Mrs. Saunders, in the early days of the *Neighborhood* program. Rogers firmly believed that in order to accept and understand the diversity of the world, children simply needed to see examples of racially diverse people coexisting in an everyday positive manner. He felt this was a particularly important idea for teachers to grasp.

"When children learn more about one another, and when they know their teachers recognize and celebrate their differences, they are more likely to feel a sense of community in the classroom. Teachers foster mutual respect when they provide activities that encourage conversation, sharing, and interaction." Realizing that he himself was a teacher of sorts, Fred tried to incorporate many child-friendly facets of the world into his neighborhood so audiences could learn about cultural and economic differences.

When the VCR came onto the market in the 1970s, allowing television viewers to record shows straight from the TV and watch them again and again, Rogers supported the technology.

"I have always felt that with the advent of all of this new technology that allows people to tape the 'Neighborhood' off-the-air…they then become much more active in the programming of their family's television life. Very frankly, I am opposed to people being programmed by others. My whole approach in broadcasting has always been 'You are an important person just the way you are. You can make healthy decisions'…I just feel that anything that allows a person to be more active in the control of his or her life, in a healthy way, is important."

Chapter Nine – Celebrity Sightings in the Neighborhood

Fred Rogers may have become a celebrity in his own right, but there was a bevy of other famous people who visited him on *Mister Rogers' Neighborhood* over the years. From actors and actresses to musicians and scientists, there was no end of talent flowing onto the *Neighborhood* set. For his part, Fred enjoyed welcoming a diverse collection of guests and showing young audiences how each celebrity was really just a normal person.

Michael Keaton, star of *Batman* (1989), found himself working on the WQED set of *Neighborhood* in the 1970s before getting his own start on the silver screen. "Where I worked…everyone who did what I did worked for Fred, eventually. I think I started at $2 an hour and was bumped up to $2.25. When you worked at [W]QED you kind of did everything. You would work on Fred's crew from time to time." Keaton even got to appear on-screen in the Neighborhood of Make-Believe dressed as a panda. In 2018, Keaton hosted the PBS 50th anniversary special, *F*RED ROGERS: AMERICA'S FAVORITE NEIGHBOR.

JULIA CHILD, ANOTHER MEMBER OF THE NET/PBS LINEUP WITH HER SHOW, THE FRENCH CHEF, DROPPED BY ROGERS' STUDIO SPACE IN 1974 TO HELP CHEF BROCKETT WHIP UP A DELICIOUS BATCH OF MARCO POLO SPAGHETTI. THE RECIPE, WHICH INCLUDES WALNUTS, OLIVES, RED PEPPERS, SWISS CHEESE, AND TUNA, HAS BEEN LOVINGLY RECREATED IN FANS' HOUSEHOLDS, ENTIRE DECADES AFTER THE EPISODE FIRST AIRED.

In 1975, Margaret Hamilton visited Mister Rogers on the show to talk about her famous role in *The Wizard of Oz*: The Wicked Witch of the West. A terrifying specter with deep green skin and an evil laugh, the Wicked Witch of the 1939 film was such an iconic figure that she remains a beloved anti-hero today. Hamilton was happy to show viewers her costume and assure children that her character wasn't real. Furthermore, she explained, the Wicked Witch wasn't really bad; she was just frustrated. She cackled that famous witchy cackle, and Rogers tried out a cackle of his own. Impressed with the character, Fred told Margaret "it would be fun to talk like that."

That same year, singer Tony Bennet dropped by to spend some time with Lady Elaine Fairchilde. Famous for songs like "Fly Me to the Moon" and "I Left My Heart in San Francisco," Bennett is less well-known for his skill with a paintbrush. While visiting the television studio inside Lady Elaine's Museum-Go-Round, Tony painted a portrait of his ladyship and sang his own version of "It's You I Like."

In 1979, Mister Rogers visited the set of *The Incredible Hulk* to meet the star of the series: Lou Ferrigno. After knocking politely on the door of a large trailer, Rogers was admitted inside to take a seat alongside a makeup team and the very scantily-clad Ferrigno. The visit was two-fold. First, Rogers wanted to show kids how Lou went from a normal human being—albeit a very large and athletic one—into the supernatural, green Hulk. Secondly, he wanted Lou to share some insights with viewers about dealing with angry feelings. Happy to comply, *The Incredible Hulk* actor explained how weight training and bodybuilding helped him deal with anger. "There's something about lifting weights that is just a tremendous release of energy from the body."

Nodding politely, the tiny-by-comparison Mister Rogers asked Lou about his childhood. "You were little once, weren't you?" Ferrigno assured Fred and his viewers that yes, he had been a little boy once, and not only that, but he suffered hearing loss at the age of three and had to learn to read lips as a child. An excited Mr. McFeely, Rogers' companion during the trip, took photos until the interview concluded.

In 1997, Mister Rogers met with another beloved children's television host, Bill Nye the Science Guy. In the final segment of Episode 1715, Bill Nye performed an experiment in Rogers' Neighborhood house to show his friend how he can blow up a balloon without using his mouth. With baking soda, vinegar, and a bottle, he did just that.

Critically acclaimed cellist Yo-Yo Ma, a Chinese-American musician who has been on stage since the age of four, was a two-time visitor to *Mister Rogers' Neighborhood*. On one occasion, Ma brought his own young son, Nicholas, to visit Mister Rogers so the two of them could perform together. With the elder Ma on cello, Nicholas took over the piano and delivered a beautiful duet. The Ma and Rogers families kept in touch regularly after these appearances and considered each other good friends.

In fact, Nicholas Ma produced the 2018 documentary on Fred Rogers, *Won't You Be My Neighbor?* with the assistance of Joanne and her two sons. Thanks to Nicholas' lifelong friendship with the family, he was able to create a biographical piece that satisfied the late Rogers' widow and sons. Though Fred's family had mostly avoided the press while he was on television, it was the collaboration of Nicholas Ma with a respectful team that convinced them to participate in the project.

Of course, it was impossible to forget who the real star of the show was, as humble and unassuming as he was. No matter who turned up in the Neighborhood, it was always Mister Rogers the kids wanted to see. Thousands of those very kids took the time to write their favorite non-parental grown-up a letter, and every one of them received a reply on *Mister Rogers' Neighborhood* letterhead. One such child by the name of Christopher wrote to tell Mister Rogers that he planned to come and visit him in the Neighborhood so they could spend some time together.

"It meant a lot to me to know that you would like to visit with me at my house. Christopher, I wish it were possible to meet with the boys and girls who want to visit, but I am busy with my work, and I need to spend my relaxing time with my family. There is also no area for guests in the studio where my television house is. Even though we can't have a real visit, it is good that we can have television visits and a letter visit like this one. You might want to pretend about a visit we'd have together. When you pretend, things can be any way you want them to be." Mister Rogers also suggested that Christopher, who had expressed a desire to play with Trolley, could make his own using a box or carton—and, of course, his imagination. Rogers closed by reminding his fan that there was no one else like him anywhere and that he was special.

Of course, fame itself meant little to Rogers unless it was used to better society—which is exactly what he hoped to do.

Chapter Ten – The Assassination of Robert Kennedy

In June of 1968, American presidential hopeful Robert Kennedy was murdered, five years after the murder of his brother, President John F. Kennedy. It was a shocking and mournful time for Americans, especially those who had supported the campaigns of both Robert and John Kennedy. Like his brother, Robert had become a stoic supporter of civil rights, and it was on a platform of equality and social justice that he campaigned for the presidency of the United States. While greeting members of hotel staff in the kitchen at the Ambassador Hotel in Los Angeles, Robert was fatally shot by a Palestinian man named Sirhan Sirhan. The killer had been outraged to hear of Kennedy's support for Israel in the ongoing territorial conflict between the Jewish state and Palestine.

As the news channels followed the story, Fred Rogers knew very well that children in the nation's households had questions that were probably going unanswered. Instead of trying to lie to children about the events going on around them, Rogers assumed that most kids throughout the country had already heard enough whispered conversations and television news to know something important was happening. Very concerned about how the violent images on TV and confusing subject matter was affecting America's youngest citizens, Fred decided to try to do something about it.

He addressed these concerns in a special episode that aired on June 7th, 1968—one day before Robert Kennedy's funeral. The episode was unnamed, and without titles, it simply faded into the interior of Mister Rogers' set living room, where the host sat formally dressed in a jacket and tie. He made no move to change into his cardigan and tennis shoes, which gave the program an air of formality. Mister Rogers was clearly addressing the parents of his usual audience members as well as kids. It was a special presentation meant to be viewed as a family—and its content would shock many who were familiar with *Mister Rogers' Neighborhood*.

Firstly, Fred acknowledged his fear that kids were in constant view and earshot of repeated footage and mentions of violence, Senator Robert Kennedy's murder, as well as from the war in Vietnam. He spoke anxiously with parents, asking them to shelter their sons and daughters from those kinds of reports and images. For a man who is notoriously composed, this particular episode reveals Rogers' emotions unlike any other. He was nervous and worried, adamant to the point of pleading that the news and gossip had to stop for the good of young people.

Fred talked solemnly to parents about how they may notice differences in the way their children are playing after hearing about the shooting. He explains that they may hide certain toys and pretend to find them again in an attempt to understand loss and death. Without the usual playful switch from house to Neighborhood of Make-Believe via the Trolley, the scene change was a straight cut onto Lady Elaine in Henrietta Pussycat's house. Excitedly, Lady Elaine chattered on about the news she had heard, a man being shot six times. After explaining, Elaine wants to play a game with X the

Owl where they both pretend to shoot each other. X, however, doesn't feel good about playing a game like that, and he talks to Lady Aberlin about it.

Lady Aberlin takes care to ensure X that making-believe something bad doesn't make it happen in real life. She explains that the man in the news who shot the other man wasn't playing a game but actually picking up a gun and using it. The make-believe characters talk about how sometimes they make bad wishes when they are angry, but those wishes don't come true and won't hurt anyone. X the Owl eventually realizes that his childhood wish to fly —which did come true—didn't turn real because of the wishing, but because he actually practiced and learned how to fly in real life.

In a later scene in the Neighborhood of Make-Believe, Rogers talks about Kennedy's murder in the guise of Daniel Striped Tiger. Daniel sits with Lady Aberlin, who is blowing up a balloon. She is surprised by Daniel's random question but handles her answer tactfully.

DANIEL STRIPED TIGER: Well, what about your air?

LADY ABERLIN: My air inside me?

DANIEL STRIPED TIGER: Mhmm. What if you blow all your air out? Then you won't have any left, just like the balloon.

LADY ABERLIN: But people aren't like balloons, Daniel. When we blow air out, we get some more back in. Watch, I'll blow air out (blowing up balloon).

DANIEL STRIPED TIGER: Oh.

LADY ABERLIN: (Blowing up balloon.)

DANIEL STRIPED TIGER: What does assassination mean?

LADY ABERLIN: (stuttering) Have you heard that word a lot today?

DANIEL STRIPED TIGER: Yes, and I didn't know what it meant.

LADY ABERLIN: Well, it means somebody getting killed in a sort of surprise way.

DANIEL STRIPED TIGER: That's what happened, you know? That man killed that other man.

LADY ABERLIN: I know, and a lot of people are talking about it right now.

DANIEL STRIPED TIGER: Too many people are talking about it.

LADY ABERLIN: A lot of people are sad and scared about it, you know?

DANIEL STRIPED TIGER: I'd rather talk about it some other day.

Back at Mister Rogers' house, the host talks about how Daniel and many other children might be confused about how a body really works and therefore harbor unwarranted fears of pain and death. He segued into the upcoming funeral for Senator Robert Kennedy, suggesting that while some families may be comforted by watching the event on television, that might not be the right decision for everybody. He wanted every family member to know that everyone deals with reality differently and it was okay to want to go for a walk instead of watching TV the next day.

It was the first time Mister Rogers felt the need to create a special episode in response to a national tragedy, but it would not be the last.

Chapter Eleven – The Famous Foot Bath

It's no secret that in the 1960s, America and many other countries were not particularly accepting toward minority groups. During a time when black Americans faced discrimination in every facet of life—from housing and jobs to restaurants and public transportation—the Civil Rights Movement took firm hold throughout the country and the world. The more that activists demanded for black Americans, the more violence there was. Lynchings, beatings, and murders of black people by whites were common as Ku Klux Klan members took it upon themselves to rid America of any people who were not of European descent.

As the 1960s progressed, the clashes between ethnic groups within the United States reached a breaking point. People were deeply divided over their beliefs concerning the future of race relations, and only with the intense devotion to the cause of peace and equality were leaders like Malcolm X and Dr. Martin Luther King Jr. able to shine a little light on a hopeful future. All black leaders, men and women, were in constant danger of violence, and in 1968, King Jr. was murdered by a white man in opposition to ethnic diversity and black rights. It was a chaotic and depressing time for many disenfranchised Americans who couldn't be sure if times would ever get better.

With very few non-white actors or presenters working on television, it became a political statement to include such people in one's program—and Fred Rogers made sure to do so. In 1968, when *Mister Rogers' Neighborhood* was just starting to air on public television, the star of the program asked a black man named François Clemmons to join his cast of human and puppet characters for a recurring role. Clemmons was part of Rogers' church, and Fred had noticed the man's robust and pleasing voice while he sang hymns. It was just the kind of talent that would find a happy home among the talented Fred and other cast members of the new children's show.

Unfortunately, Rogers' idea to cast Clemmons as a police officer in the Neighborhood of Make-Believe was a bit unsettling to a man who had grown up with a negative image of law enforcement. "I grew up in the ghetto," he told interviewers decades later. "I did not have a positive opinion of police officers. Policemen were siccing police dogs and water hoses on people," he says. "And I really had a hard time putting myself in that role. So I was not excited about being Officer Clemmons at all."

Rogers was persistent, however, and François did ultimately agree to join the cast. In doing so, he became the first black man to regularly appear on a children's show. In addition to patrolling The Land of Make-Believe as a police officer, Clemmons ran a performance and dancing studio across the street from Mister Rogers in the "real" neighborhood. He hosted many guests to the show at his studio and performed in many plays and operas put on by the characters in the program. Though he hadn't been sure about the role at first, Clemmons stayed with *Mister Rogers' Neighborhood* for 25 years, from 1968 to 1993.

The show debuted less than a month before Martin Luther King Jr. was killed; it was a time of loss and mourning for human rights activists and supporters the world over. It was also a time when America's minorities were more in need of positive examples than ever, to show them they could have a good future in what seemed a confused and daunting country. Clemmons beamed out of the television screen like a beacon to young children of all racial backgrounds. He was not only a friend of the popular host but a respected authority figure in the neighborhood. Just by wearing his policeman's uniform and interacting positively with Fred Rogers, Clemmons helped to create a more diverse mindset for generations of very young audiences. Taking the role was also a boost to François' musical career, as he was invited to participate in a variety of national musical events and was eventually appointed Artist in Residence and Director of the Martin Luther King Spiritual Choir at Vermont's Middlebury College.

On-screen with Mister Rogers, Clemmons had a particularly memorable moment during the first season of the show. It was a normal day in the neighborhood when Mister Rogers had an innocuous visit from the friendly local policeman in The Neighborhood of Make-Believe. The sun was shining bright and hot, and Fred was getting ready to soak his bare feet in a kiddie pool of water when Clemmons dropped by. Always a model neighbor, Fred invited the officer to take a bit of a break and join him. In adult circles, it was a highly controversial move, as innocent as it probably seemed to the children who watched the show. White-only clubs labeled tables and drinking fountains for whites or blacks—never both—and racist Americans of the time would have considered such a friendship downright deplorable. However, Officer Clemmons joined his friend for a quick foot soak in the cool water while the two of them chatted amiably.

It was a seemingly innocuous moment in the episode but a momentous occasion for children's television—one that would be remembered for decades to come. The neighborly, multi-racial foot bath was so popular, in fact, that it was repeated again in 1993. One last time, as Officer Clemmons, François dropped by Mister Rogers' place and enjoyed a cool soak for a few moments alongside the host of the show. Rogers requested Clemmons sing a song he had written, "Many Ways to Say I Love You," and the neighborhood officer happily complied. It was just as touching a moment as it had been the first time around—particularly because Clemmons' diversity stemmed not only from the dark color of his skin but from the fact that he was gay.

Fred Rogers had known for many years that his friend and coworker was homosexual, but it wasn't something Clemmons was allowed to show on television. He had one ear pierced as a symbol of his sexual orientation but did not wear the earring in front of PBS cameras due to Rogers' belief that homosexuality was too controversial for his show. Still, outside *Mister Rogers' Neighborhood*, François eventually came out publicly as a gay man and remained in good standing with both the show and the audience.

For Clemmons, he'll never forget the time Fred Rogers walked into the set house, hung up that iconic sweater, and sang "You make every day a special day just by being you, and I like you just the way you are" while looking right at him. François asked Rogers if he had been singing to him on purpose, and the latter replied in the affirmative.

As Clemmons recalls, Fred told him, "Yes, I have been talking to you for years. But you heard me today."

François was particularly touched. "It was like telling me I'm okay as a human being. That was one of the most meaningful experiences I'd ever had."

Chapter Twelve – PBS Funding and the Supreme Court

At the end of the 1960s, the National Education Television network (precursor to the Public Broadcasting Service) received funding of twenty million dollars per year to produce a variety of shows, *Mister Rogers' Neighborhood* among them. The now-infamous show was not alone in terms of quality PBS programming: Classic programs such as *National Geographic Specials*, *The French Kitchen*, and *Sesame Street* all debuted in the same decade on public broadcasting. Just as these programs were catching their stride, however, they faced serious contention in the form of the federal budget.

In a potentially devastating move, the federal government decided to cut its funding to public television in early 1969. As his show was aired on NET, it was important for Fred Rogers that the annual budget was not slashed; if anything, it had to be increased. It was his courage and his quiet confidence that ultimately ensured not only the continuance of his own show but every other program on NET and, in the future, PBS. Bravely, Rogers decided to go directly to the government on behalf of his colleagues at NET and other public television networks to argue the case for continued federal support.

On May 1st, 1969, Mister Rogers arrived to deliver a statement to the U.S. Senate Commerce Committee on NET funding. He arrived, dressed smartly and conservatively, to address the committee headed by Senator John O. Pastore—a man who had never heard of or seen *Mister Rogers' Neighborhood*. Though he had prepared a speech, Fred almost immediately put his statement down, explaining that it would take ten minutes to read, and he preferred to use his time to speak directly to the Senate. Even though Pastore told Rogers that he had all the time he needed to read the document, the NET advocate clearly wanted to speak frankly with his audience—as was his habit. He told the assembly that he trusted the senators would read the document afterward, then went on to describe how he believed his show was important for America's children.

"I'm constantly concerned about what our children are seeing, and for 15 years I have tried in this country and Canada, to present what I feel is a meaningful expression of care. Our program has a budget of $6000...[that] pays for less than two minutes of cartoons. Two minutes of animated, what I sometimes say, bombardment. I'm very much concerned, as I know you are, about what's being delivered to our children in this country."

Mental health was at stake, Rogers insisted, because children weren't often taught how to deal with their feelings and emotions. As his wife told interviewers years later, hers and Fred's generation were expected not to show any emotions as children or as adults. "I feel that if we in public television can only make it clear that feelings are mentionable and manageable, we will have done a great service for mental health," Rogers told the Senate, explaining that he believed all facets of emotion, especially anger, should be addressed productively.

Senator Pastore was very impressed by Rogers' passion and with the content of the *Neighborhood* program, which he asked to view as soon as possible. But Fred wasn't done making his case yet—he wanted the Senate to feel the same way he did about making each child feel special and confident. So, he shared the same words with them as he did every day with his young audience, hoping to make an emotional connection.

"This is what I give. I give an expression of care every day to each child, to help him realize that he is unique. I end the program by saying, 'You've made this day a special day, by just your being you. There's no person in the whole world like you, and I like you, just the way you are.'"

After this part of the speech, Senator Pastore confessed that he had goosebumps, which Rogers kindly thanked him for before asking to share the lyrics of his song "What Do You Do With the Mad That You Feel?" Even in the middle of the U.S. government, Fred Rogers couldn't help but express himself in song—and it worked on the Senate just as well as it did on kids.

In total, Mister Rogers spoke for a little over six minutes at the Senate hearing and held a different kind of audience captive than he was used to. His argument was rational, as he justified why what he did on children's television was more than just to mindlessly entertain with colorful animation and slapstick humor. He said they strove to give children "an expression of care every day," arguing that if people were comfortable with their emotions and expressing their feelings, the mental health of the nation would benefit from it.

"I think it's wonderful. I think it's wonderful. Looks like you just earned the $20 million," said Senator John O. Pastore once Fred was through. He wasn't exaggerating; at the conclusion of the Commerce Committee hearings, the U.S. Senate voted in favor of not only maintaining their current public television funding but increasing it. In total, the Senate gave $22 million to networks like NET over the next two years.

Fred Rogers' speech remains one of the most famous Senate speeches in U.S. history. Footage of the Senate hearing can still be found online, as can transcripts of the discourse between Rogers and Pastore. In the late 2010s, America's federal funding for PBS and other public television networks reached $445 million over a two-year period but not without continued pressure from the most recent administration to cut it entirely.

Despite a governmental body that was often ideologically split between America's dominating parties, the Republicans and the Democrats, Rogers never publicly identified with either side. Though he was a lifelong Republican, Rogers preferred to address issues on a case-by-case basis, never assuming that the individuals of each political entity would fail to listen to reason. In a 2018 interview, Joanne Rogers says of her husband, "We have somebody leading us right now who is not a forgiver. His values are very, very different from Fred's values—almost completely opposite." The future of federal television grants in the U.S. is uncertain at best.

Fortunately, PBS and its generations of viewers have not forgotten what Mister Rogers did for the burgeoning industry in 1969. He is still hailed as a hero.

Chapter Thirteen – I Don't Want to Eat Anything That Has a Mother

It's a bit of an unintentional secret, but Fred Rogers was a strict vegetarian from about the age of 45. "I don't want to eat anything that has a mother" was how he explained his vegetarianism to anyone who thought to question it. He wasn't raised on a plant-based diet, but in the early 1970s, Fred, an avid reader, read *Diet for a Small Planet* by Frances Moore Lappe and was forever changed. He wasn't alone; the book became a staple read for many people in that time period who were looking for a way to make a positive difference in the world. Like Rogers, Lappe and her readers craved a way to honor animals and the earth, while easing hunger and poverty for millions of struggling humans.

Lappe's book explained how the food industry was crippling any attempts to ease world hunger and shared statistics such as how for every seven pounds of grain fed to cattle, only one pound of meat is produced. The author promoted a plant-based diet as a way to take back one's individual power from the endless influence of advertising and the status quo. Rogers, like Lappe, was appalled at the careless and violent ways in which farmed animals were treated, and he renounced all types of meat for good.

"I want to be a vehicle for God, to spread his message of love and peace," Rogers said, believing that by rejecting slaughtered animals as food, he was doing what God would advise. At the time, few Christians and non-Christians followed a vegetarian lifestyle, let alone knew what one was. His was a lonely path for a long time in regards to food, but Rogers persevered. Not only did he forego the violence of the meat industry, but he was actively protesting the use of nourishing grains and vegetables to fatten animals destined for the slaughterhouse. For the good of the earth, mankind, and his own peace of mind, Rogers never ate meat again. He once said that it was difficult to eat anything you'd seen walking around.

In fact, he became the co-owner of *Vegetarian Times* magazine in 1985 when he helped his friend Jeff Obis, editor and founder of the magazine, buy it back from Associated Business Publications. As a minority shareholder in the only large-scale magazine of its kind during the 1980s and 90s, Rogers' financial contribution allowed Obis to resell *Vegetarian Times* to Cowles Media for a reported $10 million. It was a financial win for both men and a way to keep the magazine going for another 20 years.

The November 1983 issue of *Vegetarian Times* featured Fred Rogers himself on the cover with the caption "The Surprising Fred Rogers, America's Favorite Neighbor." In a detailed interview, Rogers told the magazine that he had witnessed many children become concerned at the realization that animals and food were connected. To him, this was likely further proof that giving up meat was the right thing to do. In an average day, Rogers told *Vegetarian Times*, he would eat toast and fruit, yogurt and more fruit, then tofu and vegetables, also professing a love of tofu burgers and beets. When asked about what he thought of children's diets, Rogers admitted he didn't think sugary snacks were a good idea, stating that he wished kids could enjoy a variety of fruits, nuts, and vegetables instead.

In Episode 1606, Rogers had a chance to show his audience the amazing beauty of real animals when he went to visit the Neighborhood Wild Animal Park. There, he looked at giraffes, water birds, and tigers with the park guide, learning how to treat the animals with respect and admiration. Back in the Neighborhood of Make-Believe, Chef Brockett prepared a vegetable tray.

Though he didn't eat the same diet as most, Mister Rogers never came out and said as much on camera. If you looked carefully, however, all the signs were there. Throughout the entire series of *Mister Rogers Neighborhood*, Fred presents many mini-documentaries and special segments explaining where food comes from—and not one of them include animals or meat. Instead, Rogers showcased applesauce, soy products, vegetable gardening, and a variety of other plant-based meals. In Episode 1537, when Rogers sang "What Do You Do With the Mad That You Feel?" he also received a package of tofu from Mr. McFeely before making granola for the neighbors. In Episode 1539, he shows viewers a book about vegetables and talks about how people put different vegetables together to make soup before taking them to tour a factory that makes soup.

In a 1997 interview with Candace A. Wedlan of the *Sun-Sentinel*, Fred confessed that he didn't put much thought into what he ate—though, that apparent "little" thought always came up with a meal that was meat-free and decidedly nutritious. Partial to granola and milk, Rogers avoided tea and coffee and had a habit of heating up his fruit juice in the microwave. "I love pasta, mostly angel hair. And vegetables and lentil burgers. People often ask me about the vegetarian business. I think that I was a vegetarian long before it was fashionable."

Still today, most people who watched *Mister Rogers' Neighborhood* and read Rogers' many books don't realize that their idol was a vegetarian. What they do tend to notice, however, was Rogers' trim figure and affection for fruits and vegetables. The man himself claimed a beneficial side-effect to being a vegetarian was that he rarely put on weight, noting that on most days he weighed 143 pounds. It was a special number to Rogers, one that he used to say means "I love you," due to there being 1 letter in "I," four letters in "love," and 3 letters in "you."

In maintaining that weight, in part by being an active swimmer and keeping an animal-free diet, Rogers seemed to feel that all his choices had come full circle, for the good of himself and those he inspired.

Chapter Fourteen – Mister Rogers Goes to Sesame Street

Mister Rogers' Neighborhood shared the PBS children's programming spotlight with another top-rated show everyone adored: Sesame Street. Both shows got their start in the late 1960s on PBS, and both were instant hits with children and their families. Following the decision of the Supreme Court to provide generous funding to public television, *Sesame Street* benefited right along with *Mister Rogers'*. Fans of each show drew comparisons between Rogers' use of puppets and matter-of-fact conversation with Sesame Street's combination of Muppets and pleasant-mannered human characters. Both shows targeted children between the ages of two and five and made it a priority to provide educational content.

The similarities of the two shows weren't lost on the producers and actors working on *Mister Rogers'* or *Sesame Street,* and in 1981, they decided to shoot two crossover episodes, one on each set. The first featured a surprise Mister Rogers sighting on *Sesame Street* during Episode 1575, in May of that same year. While Big Bird and his friend Mr. Snuffleupagus were getting ready to race one another, they realized they would need someone to judge the result. As Big Bird looked all around his neighborhood in search of a volunteer, he saw a familiar face that made him do a double-take: it was the one and only Fred Rogers, dressed for success in a beige suit. Big Bird couldn't quite place the friendly man, but he gladly accepted his help in judging the race.

The results are clear as day when Big Bird crosses the finish line way ahead of his big, slow friend. In fact, Mr. Snuffleupagus took so long to come to the end of the race that Mister Rogers had to leave before meeting him. When Big Bird excitedly told his friend who he had just met, Snuffy didn't believe him. Unsure how to deal with his feelings, Big Bird said to another friend, "It was the most exciting day of my life, and I don't want to talk about it!" Later in the same episode, Mister Rogers visited Big Bird at his nest, and the two discussed the difference between seeing something in your imagination versus seeing it in reality.

Imagination versus reality was an ongoing point of contention between the normally gentle and accommodating Mister Rogers and Big Bird, the latter acted by Caroll Spinney. Whereas Rogers made a concerted effort to draw a line between fantasy and reality on his show, he felt that the Muppet world of Sesame Street failed to explain itself properly to the audience. So, when Spinney was due to visit the set of *Mister Rogers' Neighborhood*, he was shocked to see that Rogers' script called for him to take off the Big Bird suit and show viewers just how it all worked.

Such a move would ruin the magic of Big Bird, Spinney argued— assumedly in polite tones. Though he was willing to see Rogers' point of view, he wasn't prepared to expose the costume that was his beloved Sesame Street character. Spinney admitted later that the two of them had a very serious phone discussion about it that lasted no less than twenty minutes. In the end, they decided to have Big Bird remain intact so long as his visit was confined to the Neighborhood of Make-Believe. There, Rogers posited, the Muppet was free to be himself since all the characters and locations within Make-Believe were imaginary—a fact Rogers' viewers already knew.

The encounter aired in June of 1981 in Episode 1483. As worked out between Spinney and Rogers, Big Bird did indeed make his *Mister Rogers' Neighborhood* debut in the Neighborhood of Make-Believe, in which it was revealed that he was a friend of X the Owl. The two spent some time together and talked about the Draw the Neighborhood Contest being held that day. Big Bird had an oversized drawing of his own to contribute, but Lady Elaine Fairchilde, determined to win the contest for herself, told him it didn't fit the size requirements. Henrietta Pussycat, a close friend to X Owl, worried that Big Bird had more in common with X and would therefore be a better friend. Worried and jealous, Henrietta was the only member of the Neighborhood of Make-Believe that acted unwelcoming to the big yellow bird, since everyone else prepared welcome signs with Big Bird's face on them. In the end, they all decided to be friends, and Big Bird assured Henrietta Pussycat that he had no intentions of friend-stealing.

Rogers, however, still managed to get in his personal two cents on the legitimacy of Big Bird, donning a long-necked giraffe costume shorty before Big Bird's arrival and showing viewers how people could be transformed into big creatures that were "just pretend." All controversy aside, the crossover episodes were a hit with children, and they remain two of the most popular episodes of both programs. The exchange was a success, but the two shows didn't attempt a follow-up despite the fact that they both continued side-by-side for another two decades. There are a few moments in Sesame Street when Mister Rogers is mentioned after 1981, however.

Bert—of Bert and Ernie fame—was once seen writing a letter to Mister Rogers, and on the record, *Big Bird Discovers the Orchestra*, Big Bird decided to take the time to go help a friend even though it was time for *Mister Rogers'* on television. In Sesame Street Episode 4088, which aired two years after Rogers' death, Mr. Snuffleupagus wishes he could float like a cloud. In answer to his wish, the Fairy

Balloon Person drops by and gives him enough balloons to carry him up into the sky. When the wish is granted, there is the sound of a jingling bell. The fairy listens, explaining that he hears another wish. "SOMEBODY IN MISTER ROGERS' NEIGHBORHOOD WANTS A BALLOON. I BET IT'S A BEAUTIFUL DAY THERE!"

Chapter Fifteen – Mister Rogers the Composer

Everyone knows that Fred Rogers loved to sing, but it's easy to forget that his college degree was for composition. The songs sung by Rogers, his puppets, and guests on *Mister Rogers' Neighborhood* were actually written by Fred, including the mini-operas performed on several episodes of the show. His love of piano and song never wavered from when he was a child, making *Neighborhood* a largely musical—if somewhat subtly so—program.

Though his first work on NBC's musical programs was directly in line with Rogers' college education at Rollins, the switch to children's programming seemed to have much less to do with music. That is until Fred's own personality immediately became a part of the show. Right from the word "go," Rogers got to work writing songs for his own scripts, performing them personally in front of the camera. They were short, simple, and memorable—perfect for the young audiences Fred and his producers hoped to inspire. Rogers' intuition was on target, as his songwriting and singing became a

fixed feature of his early work as well as *Mister Rogers'*
Neighborhood.

Mister Rogers' most famous composition is unquestionably the
opening song to *Neighborhood*:

It's a beautiful day in this neighborhood

A beautiful day for a neighbor

Would you be mine?

Could you be mine?

It's a neighborly day in this beauty wood

A neighborly day for a beauty

Would you be mine?

Could you be mine?

I have always wanted to have a neighbor just like you

I've always wanted to live in a neighborhood with you

So, let's make the most of this beautiful day

Since we're together we might as well say:

Would you be mine?

Could you be mine?

Won't you be my neighbor?

Won't you please

Won't you please?

Please won't you be my neighbor?

You help to make each day a special day

By just your being yourself

There's nobody else in the whole world who's exactly like you

And people can like you exactly as you are.

Even people who did not grow up watching Mister Rogers on television can still recognize these lyrics, automatically imagining a smiling Rogers putting on his cardigan and tennis shoes after walking into his set living room. His fans remember many of the show's songs, including "It's You I Like" and "What Do You Do With the Mad That You Feel?"

Most college graduates with a degree in musical composition probably don't dream of entertaining children with their songs, but for Fred Rogers, that was exactly what made him feel like a productive and important member of society and the television industry. Amazingly, Rogers composed more than two hundred songs over the course of his career and released twelve children's music albums.

He didn't stop there, either. Included as part of his regular *Neighborhood* shows were nine complete children's operas, each about 20–30 minutes in length. Rogers explained to his young audience in episode 1475 that "an opera is like a story you sing," before introducing "an opera called Wind Storm in Bubble Land." In this particular opera, Lady Elaine—playing the part of a hummingbird in a news team—reports an incoming wind storm that threatens to blow all of Bubble Land's bubbles away. The other reporters don't believe her, however, because as they say, "We don't want to!" The story unfolds in a series of songs that lead the brave and resourceful hummingbird to save the day, flapping her wings against the storm and teaching everyone else to do the same.

These operas were the self-contained musical and dramatic masterpieces of the *Mister Rogers' Neighborhood* program, and they gave Fred the opportunity to really stretch his creative wings outside of the usual show structure and put his musical education to work. They also gave young audiences the chance to lose themselves in what was essentially a unique story as told by their beloved regular *Mister Rogers'* characters. Everyone from Officer Clemmons to Daniel Striped Tiger performed in these rare operas, taking on the persona of a new character while retaining enough of their normal appearance to be recognizable.

As creative and naturally empathetic as he was, Rogers didn't just write songs on a whim. Much of the time, he conferred with Margaret McFarland, a child psychologist with the University of Pittsburgh, to create songs that were both memorable and helpful to children. McFarland, born in 1905 in Oakdale, Pennsylvania, specialized in researching the interactions and relationships between children and their mothers. She and Rogers met during the latter's time at seminary school when her presence was requested to supervise his work with a child for a counseling session that was part of Fred's curriculum. Their beliefs on children's education and entertainment meshed extremely well, and a decade later, Margaret was asked to become a consultant for *Mister Rogers' Neighborhood*.

In addition to McFarland's input on the song content, Rogers worked regularly with a jazz band who accompanied his voice throughout each episode. Joe Negri played guitar, Carl McVicker Jr. played bass guitar, Bobby Rawsthorne took care of the percussion, and Johnny Costa played piano and directed the musical selections. Of course, the house band and Mister Rogers weren't the only musical performers on the show. International greats like the cellist Yo-Yo Ma and pianist Van Cliburn visited the *Neighborhood* from time to time to perform a song or two for Mister Rogers and company. Each visiting musical talent finished his or her performance with a rendition of one of Mister Rogers' own songs, which the children could sing along with.

Each musical piece performed on *Neighborhood,* either by Rogers and the set band or a special guest, was slow in tempo and easy for young ears and voices to follow along. Rogers wanted his audience to fully comprehend the music and like what they were hearing. Said Joe Negri of his former colleague:

"He wanted the kids to hear quality."

Chapter Sixteen – The Conflict Series

In the 1980s, the United States of America was in a state of extreme tension with the U.S.S.R. because of the two country's very different economic approaches. While America practiced and wholeheartedly propagandized the merits of democracy, the U.S.S.R. did the same with communism. Both countries were two of the richest and largest nations in the world, and though the two had been careful allies during World War II, their mutual animosity carried on after 1945. The rivalry became so acute by the 1980s that the world feared one would attack the other with a nuclear strike. Until the situation was resolved, it was referred to as the Cold War—a battle in which no bombs were dropped.

Fred Rogers was indeed a gentle man, but he was never one to shy away from the truth as it pertained to children. At the height of the Cold War, in the mid-1980s, he felt an urgent need to help his viewers understand a little bit of what was happening—and what could potentially happen—between two different communities who lived at a distance from each other. So, in the first part of Rogers' 1983 *Mister Rogers' Neighborhood* season, he scripted and filmed five special episodes that were dubbed the "Conflict Series." They originally ran from November 7th to 11th.

It all started in the Neighborhood of Make-Believe when King Friday XIII heard a rumor about the nearby town of Southwood. It seemed that Cornflake S. Pecially, the rocking chair maker otherwise known as Corny, had been commissioned to create an unprecedentedly large order of some new parts for Southwood—but no one could understand just what those parts were supposed to do. Concerned, King Friday decides he should make an order of the same parts for his own kingdom. When Handyman Negri goes to Corny to buy a sample, he discovers they are pretty expensive. Corny says that might be so, but the people of Southwood are sure willing to pay that price for the parts they need.

In Episode 1522, the second in the conflict series, the King decides the mysterious parts must be for Southwood to produce bombs and attack its neighbors—namely the Neighborhood of Make-Believe. Alarmed, Friday sets to work making his own bombs from Corny's special pieces. The next three episodes show how the characters of King Friday XIII's community process their own worry over the potential bombs and then become upset at the fact that bombs are being made in their own neighborhood. Adamant that the people of Southwood are peaceful, Lady Elaine Fairchilde and Lady Aberlin travel to the nearby town to see what exactly is happening. As it turned out, Southwood was buying all those parts to put together a nice new bridge—and all King Friday needed to do was talk to them about it, instead of letting his fear get the better of him.

In the final episode of the conflict series, the Neighborhood of Make-Believe had a peace festival to which the people of Southwood were invited. Mister Rogers himself sang "Peace and Quiet." In a very rare move for the quiet Presbyterian minister, Rogers included text from the Bible on-screen just before the show came to an end. It was obviously meant for his adult audience members.

AND THEY SHALL BEAT THEIR SWORDS INTO PLOWSHARES,

AND THEIR SPEARS INTO PRUNING FORKS;

NATION SHALL NOT LIFT UP SWORD AGAINST NATION,

NEITHER SHALL THEY LEARN WAR ANY MORE.

These episodes went into PBS' regular circulation just like all *Mister Rogers' Neighborhood* episodes, but in 1996, they were deleted from the archive because of content pertaining to war and violence. All five episodes were lost to fans, but in 2017, a few were uploaded to YouTube. As of this writing, some can still be seen on Archive.com.

Chapter Seventeen – When Fred Met Koko

In 1998, Rogers had the chance to meet a very unique fan who was born at the San Francisco Zoo. She was 27 years old and had spent most of her life in California at The Gorilla Foundation's preserve in the mountains of Santa Cruz. Her name was Koko, and she was a western lowland gorilla famous for her ability to communicate with humans using sign language. In Episode 1727, Mister Rogers took his viewers along to meet the famous gorilla and see just what she might have to say.

It was an opportunity that few people would have the honor of receiving, as Koko was probably the most famous gorilla in the world. She had been raised in captivity at the Foundation and taught from infancy to understand English words and speak using modified American Sign Language. Given Koko's celebrity status, she had the chance to meet several of her own heroes, including Betty White, Leonardo DiCaprio, Robin Williams, and of course, Mister Rogers.

Like millions of humans her age, Koko had been watching Mister Rogers on television since she was just a little baby. Her caretakers told their visitor that she was very excited to meet him. Rogers assured them that he was every bit as delighted to meet Koko as she was him. Both the *Mister Rogers' Neighborhood* crew and the sanctuary filmed the encounter and took photos, both publishing several clips of the meeting. Immediately upon seeing Fred, the gorilla was visibly excited, motioning for the gate to her special room to be opened. "Hurry," she signed to Penny Patterson, the woman who taught her sign language. She was clearly impatient to join the people in the main part of the sanctuary building. As soon as the lock was unfastened, Koko pushed the door open herself and lumbered out to greet her visitor.

Immediately, Koko took Rogers' bag and rifled through it, removing a Daniel Striped Tiger toy. She took her visitor's hand and sniffed it before unzipping his green cardigan and beckoning to him to come and see her room—just like young people do when they receive a visit from a friend. Rogers praised Koko for knowing what to do with a zipper and followed her into the space where she spent most of her time. While they sat, the inquisitive Koko wanted to know what the "flower" on Mister Rogers' shirtsleeve was—it turned out to be a sun-shaped cufflink, a gift from Fred's grandfather. "It does look like a flower," Rogers conceded kindly, and Koko signed "love" several times.

The fully-grown Koko dwarfed the six-foot and lanky Fred, easily positioning him right in her lap for closer inspection. Perhaps a little intimidated and determined to convey his friendship to Koko, Rogers let the 280-pound gorilla have her way. She made a growling sound which Penny assured Fred was a good thing. "Is it?" he replied with a comical catch in his voice. He chatted sweetly with the gorilla while she held him tightly, almost as if Rogers was a brand-new pet. He didn't seem to mind.

With the help of Penny, Fred and Koko had a friendly and successful visit. In particular, the gorilla enjoyed playing with her new friend's harmonica and camera. She snapped photo after photo on the classic film camera before finally handing it back and having her own picture taken with Penny and Fred. Koko even instigated a game of peek-a-boo with a blanket covered in pictures of cats—her favorite animal. Penny was surprised to see that the adult gorilla remembered this game, as they must not have played it in some time.

Said Rogers, as part of his television episode, "She became so interested in me that she wanted to see what was under my shoes and socks. I remember how well she used those hands of hers—even to tickle!" For the benefit of his viewers, a video played once more of Koko and Mister Rogers together, the gorilla deftly removing her visitor's shoes and pulling at his socks. When Fred's feet were bare, Koko stuck her own foot against his to compare.

"When you like someone, you want to know all you can about that someone. Especially when he has things you're not used to seeing," Mister Rogers said cheerfully, explaining the scene later in his studio. He told viewers how happy he was that people like Penny existed, who took the time to learn so much about animals like Koko. "Gorillas are very special beings," he concluded, before taking a toy gorilla he had brought in for the episode and bringing it over to the Trolley track. That day, the Neighborhood of Make-Believe had its own gorilla encounter.

Koko died in her sleep at the age of 46 in 2018. She had lived a slightly longer life than that of the average wild gorilla and outlived her friend Fred Rogers by 15 years.

Chapter Eighteen – Fred Retires from the Neighborhood

In 2001, the last episode of *Mister Rogers' Neighborhood* was broadcast. After 895 episodes, the most beloved of all children's television hosts decided it was time to take off his work shoes and put on his sneakers with his television friends and neighbors one last time. What he had ensured throughout his career was that he was adding to a library that would be around when he wasn't—his episodes were archived with PBS and could be replayed for coming generations who could use his guidance.

The final episode of *Mister Rogers' Neighborhood* aired on August 31st, 2001. It was the fifth episode of the shortest season of the program, in which Fred and his cast of characters explored the arts. In the Neighborhood of Make-Believe, there was an unprecedented twist as King Friday XIII's art festival led to a personal revelation for the grumpy Lady Elaine Fairchilde. It was Fred's way of wrapping up some loose ends in the world he had created and shared with children for so long.

In Rogers' last few visits to the Land of Make-Believe over the course of the 32nd and final season of the show, puppets and human characters gathered to display their artwork: Chuck Aber and Hula Mouse created a sand sculpture, while Lady Aberlin performed a dance and Daniel Striped Tiger made a little mobile. Throughout the episodes, Lady Elaine Fairchilde was her usual self, declaring that only she can be the judge of the art competition so the competitors will be critiqued properly.

Certainly one of the world's most critical and confident puppets, Lady Elaine spent her entire *Neighborhood* career second-guessing the rest of the cast. In the final episode, however, she judged all the artwork equally, displaying them together as a collage instead of picking a winner. At long last, she had learned to place the opinions and work of all her friends and companions at the same value. The participants celebrated together, and that's how we left them, presumably continuing their make-believe lives happily ever after.

As for Fred Rogers, he made it clear that though the show was over, he wasn't finished working. He still had projects to do with his company, Family Communications, Inc. Working with fifteen staff members, including David Newell—who played Mr. McFeely on the show—Rogers looked for ways to use the internet to continue spreading his message and educate kids. In his small office, Rogers dropped the cardigan in favor of a suit jacket and bow tie like his grandfather wore, ready to move from television and into the virtual world of the internet. His website at **www.MisterRogers.org** was already well underway, filled with advice for parents on a range of topics that included potty training and playing games. Today, that website is an homage to the man himself and the world he created on *Mister Rogers' Neighborhood*.

According to his wife, Fred was happy to move on from the show he had put so much effort into. Joanne Rogers told Doreen Carvajal of *The New York Times* that though her husband probably missed working in the Neighborhood of Make-Believe, he had come to dread taping the interior scenes where he was alone, introducing and concluding each show. Fred personally told the press that over time he disliked the need for television makeup and contact lenses, as he preferred just to present himself as-is. In the early days, he explained, there was no need for all that. Still proud of his accomplishments with *Mister Rogers' Neighborhood*, of course, Rogers had simply come to feel that he had done all he could with the show. It was time for him to focus on other projects that had been accumulating in his brain.

Though Fred was finished with the *Neighborhood*, he tried for some time to find a new host to replace him on the show and keep it going. Of course, it had to be someone like Rogers—someone who treasured children but wanted to be frank and truthful with them as well. He or she needed to have the same values as Rogers but understand how to restrain themselves from preaching or talking down to the audience. Perhaps, he thought, it could be someone who grew up watching the show. In the end, his quiet search amounted to nobody, and everyone had to accept that the show was truly coming to an end.

Having given his show archives to the university of pittsburgh, fred moved on. He discussed creating an online stream of bedtime stories with his family communications team. While the technicians worked out the logistics of that enterprise, rogers turned once more to the old-fashioned form of storytelling: writing books. He had already been writing parenting books and children's stories since the 1980s, including a series called first experiences. First experiences explored scary or complicated situations that every child has to face, such as visiting the dentist, and explains them so they aren't quite as scary. After retirement, fred authored two more books aimed at parents: the mister rogers' parenting book: *Helping to Understand Your Young Child* and *Mister Rogers' Playtime*. The first emphasized the joy and growth that comes to adults who are parents; the second included 80 games and activities for parents with children aged 3–7.

Apart from writing books and exploring the possibilities of online broadcasts, Rogers maintained his daily swimming routine and happily checked the scale after each session for the numbers "143." He continued to eat well and spend his extra time with his family, which had grown to include grandchildren. The family spent time together at their summer house in Nantucket, enjoying the scenery and sunshine together. In his own mind, of course, Fred wasn't fully retired. He kept his eyes and ears open, just in case he might be needed on-screen once more. In fact, just a few months after his last episode aired, Rogers deemed it absolutely necessary to get in front of the television camera and speak to the public.

On September 11th, 2001, two hijacked airplanes were flown into the World Trade Center towers in New York City. A third airplane struck the Pentagon in Washington, D.C, and a fourth crashed into a field in Pennsylvania. Almost 3,000 people were killed in the attacks, which immediately grounded all US flights and sent Americans into a panic. A radical Islamic leader by the name of Osama bin Laden claimed responsibility for the attacks, stating that this was America's punishment for its support of Israel in the ongoing Middle Eastern conflicts. It was the same justification that had been used 33 years earlier when Sirhan Sirhan shot and killed Senator Robert Kennedy.

Rogers taped multiple short clips aimed at parents, whom he knew must be wondering what to say to their kids at such a tragic and frightening time. Seated at the piano in his *Neighborhood* set, Mister Rogers explained that "What children probably need to hear most from us, as adults, is that they can talk to us about anything. And that we will do all we can to keep them safe, in any scary time." He played a thoughtful tune on the keys as the scene faded out. It was just a quick and succinct piece of advice from a trusted friend—a friend with an awful lot of experience dealing gently with children during times of tragedy and violence.

Back in 1981, even before the Conflict series aired, Fred had reason to make a special announcement on-air after the murder of former Beatle, John Lennon, as well as the attempted assassination of U.S. President Ronald Reagan. In Rome that same year, there was a failed assassination attempt on Pope John Paul II. So, in a special broadcast, Mister Rogers told his viewers that this time they needed to watch the show with an adult they trusted because he was going to be talking about sad and scary things. On-screen, Rogers talked with real children about how they were feeling and reacting to things they heard and saw on the news. Then he spoke personally about events and explained how some people are very angry and sick, and they feel like the only way to feel better is to do terrible things.

Not only was Rogers' approach unique in its truthfulness, but it was different in that he never affixed labels like "good guy" and "bad guy" on anyone. Violence and anger were complex issues that should be treated as such, as far as he was concerned, and he didn't want to give kids the impression that people were polarized as good and bad. It was in this special broadcast that Rogers told viewers what his own mother used to tell him in troubling times: To look for the helpers any time there is trouble and realize that there is always someone on the scene to provide assistance to those in need. It was a tidbit he repeated often in interviews, stating that he wished news coverage of live events would take more time to show medical, police, and fire teams coming in to deal with the situation. "If you see the helpers, you know there is hope."

Chapter Nineteen – Satire and Criticism

As beloved and popular as *Mister Rogers' Neighborhood* was during its more than three-decade run, it and its sweet, docile host became the subject of much parody and caricature over the course of Fred Rogers' life. Perhaps Fred was an easy target, but sometimes even he was a fan of the mimicry of his personality and show on television and radio. In an interview with David Letterman in 1982, Rogers admitted that some of the satire didn't sit well with him, but when the skits were performed out of affection, he thought they were a precious tribute.

Johnny Carson did an adult version of the show in 1978, in which he perfectly mimicked the way in which Mister Rogers enters his home, exchanges his work jacket for a comfortable cardigan, and does the same with his work shoes and sneakers. Carson goaded his fake audience into purchasing a club membership to be his friend and then used dolls to act out a scene in which Mommy Doll and Daddy Doll make a baby. Carson was a huge celebrity at the time and is unlikely to have been using Rogers' persona to make any actual critique; nevertheless, the skit did draw some criticism from fans who wanted to keep Rogers' innocent character untouched by brash adult realism.

On the late-night comedy skit show, *Saturday Night Live*, Rogers also found himself ripe for the picking by cast member Eddie Murphy. Between 1981 and 1984, Murphy dressed up like Rogers nine times and introduced "Mister Robinson's Neighborhood," a poor inner-city slum. Upbeat, calm, and endearing like the host he parodied, Murphy gently introduced his audience to real-life topics like poverty, joblessness, and burglary. Most of all, he used the innocent premise of Rogers' show to highlight how different American life was for a lot of black people like himself.

In one episode, the introductory song lyrics from the real *Mister Rogers' Neighborhood* show were slightly tweaked to suit the *Saturday Night Live* set. Murphy sang: "It's one hell of a day in the neighborhood. A hell of a day for a neighbor! Would you be mine? Could you be mine? I hope I get to move into the neighborhood someday. The problem is, when I move in, y'all move away!"

When the doorbell rang in the set apartment—a classic *Mister Rogers'* plot point—instead of a friendly visitor, it was the landlord with an eviction notice. After the landlord left, Murphy introduced "Scumbucket" as the special word of the day, explaining that even if his audience members weren't familiar with the word, they almost certainly knew someone who fit the description.

Eddie Murphy didn't stop there. He also put his own spin on the make-believe portion of Rogers' show, voicing and maneuvering his own puppets. In Robinson's Magical Land of Make-Believe, a variety of black finger puppets asked a President Reagan doll why he couldn't provide school lunches or help the poor. The doll ran away.

As it turned out, Fred Rogers not only watched the episodes of "Mister Robinson's Neighborhood," but he liked them a lot. He even went to the set of *Saturday Night Live* in 1982 and knocked on Eddie

Murphy's dressing room door to surprise him. They had a friendly meeting and a Polaroid photo taken of the two of them together, which Murphy signed. It was a story that Rogers loved to tell.

Not everyone who used Mister Rogers as subject matter for their own work was a fan, however. Lawrence Diller is just one medical practitioner who published a very adamant critique of the nurture method of child-rearing. In his 2006 book, *The Last Normal Child: Essays on the Intersection of Kids, Culture, and Psychiatric Drugs*, Diller insisted that focusing on a child's emotions and self-confidence so much—as Mister Rogers always did, saying on every episode of his show that everyone is special—had created a generation of wimps. Diller wrote an article for *Psychology Today* in 2008, in which he supported the claims of Charles McGrath, book reviewer for *The New York Times*:

Wrote McGrath:

"Some of us have raised dummies and the disengaged not on purpose, surely, but perhaps because we listened to Mr. Rogers and told them too often that we liked them just the way they were."

More criticism for the cherished children's television presenter has reared its head in the last decade, centered around Rogers' classic advice to children to "look for the helpers" in times of tragedy. It was a theme he talked about often: "To this day, especially in times of 'disaster,' I remember my mother's words and I am always comforted by realizing that there are still so many helpers — so many caring people in this world."

From those who had always found comfort in Mister Rogers' calm, confident presence, the quotation was recalled to help survivors of the Sandy Hook Elementary School shooting in 2012. As school shootings became a regular occurrence in the United States, "Look for the helpers" has been quoted more and more often, prompting criticism for its continued use. With so much tragedy, and therefore perhaps an overwhelming use of Mister Rogers' innocent, helpful words, some people have a negative reaction to the quotation. Don't just look for the helpers, they urge. Be a helper. That's what adults do.

Indeed, with so many people having grown up with Mister Rogers' words in their ears whenever the world seemed scary, it does seem natural to recall the things he said now. It is also true, however, that *Mister Rogers' Neighborhood* was written and presented for the benefit of children; so as a generation of adults and parents, it has become his audience's turn to be the helpers their children can look up to. Sadly, childhood in America is quite different today than it was when Rogers' show premiered on television, and that's a fact that lends itself to criticism of his gentle methods.

It's probably not wrong to assume that Fred Rogers himself would have something comforting to say now, both to adults and children. As the man himself wrote in his book, *You Are Special: Neighborly Wit And Wisdom From Mister Rogers*,

> We live in a world in which we need to share responsibility. It's easy to say 'It's not my child, not my community, not my world, not my problem.' Then there are those who see the need and respond. I consider those people my heroes.

Chapter Twenty – Illness and Death

Less than two years after his retirement from *Mister Rogers' Neighborhood*, Fred Rogers fell seriously ill with stomach cancer. It was a quick illness, and though Rogers underwent surgery to try to extend his life in January of 2003, he died on February 27th at his Pittsburgh home. Joanne, by then married to Fred for 50 years, was with him.

Knowing that he may not recover from his illness, Rogers went into the recording studio in the latter part of 2002 and taped a message for all his fans—many of whom he knew were quite grown up. He wasn't saying goodbye but simply sending a message out into a world of people he had helped raise and telling everyone he was proud of what they'd accomplished.

In the video, Fred sat at the piano in his studio in a jacket, tie, and glasses. He smiled naturally and told his audience a story about how adults aged 20 to 40 often approached him in public, eager to meet

Mister Rogers and thank him for his show. These people, Rogers explained, often told him about how they learned the importance of expressing themselves creatively from his show, and now they funnel that passion into writing, dance, computers, and many other professional fields.

"I'm just so proud of all of you who have grown up with us," he said. "I know how tough it is, some days, to look with hope and confidence on the months and years ahead. But I would like to tell you what I often told you when you were much younger. I like you just the way you are. And what's more, I'm so grateful to you for helping the children in your life, to know that you'll do everything you can to keep them safe...it's such a good feeling to know that we're lifelong friends." At that, Mister Rogers smiled, and the image of his familiar face faded to black.

One of Rogers' red cardigans, knitted by his mother Nancy, is now owned by the Smithsonian National Museum of American History in Washington, D.C. It was a personal gift from Fred.

Chapter Twenty-One – Awards and Legacy

A life like the one led by Fred McFeely Rogers doesn't go unnoticed. Those 33 years spent in children's television not only fostered a loyal group of fans in many age groups, but it earned Fred Rogers a reputation as a respected champion of children's education. His show received four Emmy Awards, and in 1997, he received the Lifetime Achievement Award at the Daytime Emmy Awards. Despite never having intended to find fame, Rogers was too beloved and ingrained in the social fabric of America not to be celebrated; he received awards and acknowledgments his entire career.

As early as 1975, Fred received a Ralph Lowell Award for outstanding contributions to, or achievements in, public television. Named for a Boston philanthropist, the Ralph Lowell Award is gifted annually by the Corporation for Public Broadcasting. It was the first time that Fred had been publicly congratulated for his work in children's entertainment, but it was far from the last. In 1986 and 1987, *Mister Rogers' Neighborhood* won the CINE Golden Eagle award for children's programming and also given honorary membership to the Phi Mu Alpha Sinfonia Fraternity of America—an all-male brotherhood committed to the advancement of music in the United States.

Not only was he awarded for his creative work, but Rogers was credited with playing the role of "himself" in hosting *Neighborhood*. The Daytime Emmy Awards hailed him an outstanding performer and awarded the show the prize for Outstanding Individual Achievement in Children's Programming in 1980, then for Outstanding Writing in a Children's Series in 1985. Every year from 1980 to 2003, Rogers and his show were nominated for a Daytime Emmy. In 1997, Rogers not only won another one of the awards but was given the Lifetime Achievement Award. It was a touching moment not only for Fred but for the audience at the awards ceremony. Before walking up to the stage in his handsome black tuxedo, Rogers kissed his wife Joanne, and they both smiled at the cameras. When the standing ovation and applause died down, he spoke earnestly to the crowd.

"Oh, it's a beautiful night in this neighborhood," he said, and the audience laughed. "So many people have helped me to come to this night...All of us have special ones who have loved us into being. Would you just take—along with me—ten seconds to think of the people who have helped you become who you are?"

Fred looked at his watch and silently counted down the seconds while the audience did as he requested. Many held back tears. At the end of the silence, Rogers spoke kindly of all the wonderful people who must have been in the crowd's imagination. He thanked his family and colleagues and said "May God be with you" before exiting the stage. As always, he was soft-spoken, eloquent, and not inclined to say any more than was necessary to the occasion. And like so many times before, he left his audience with a feeling of happiness and tranquility.

It wouldn't have surprised those who knew him well that Fred didn't just want to receive awards but give them to others as well. In 1994, Fred hosted a television special called *Fred Rogers' Heroes: Who's Helping America's Children.* The heroes featured on the program were Glojean Todacheene, a Navajo schoolteacher at a First Nations reservation in Shiprock, New Mexico; Olomenji O'Connor, creator of Project Peace to promote non-violence among Chicago's public housing children; Carola De La Rocha, dance teacher in Los Angeles, California; and Dr. Samuel Ross, founder of residential children's trauma treatment center, Green Chimneys, in New York state.

To those being honored for their hands-on contributions to the nation's youth, Rogers said:

> Most of my childhood heroes wore capes, flew through the air, and picked up buildings with one arm. They were spectacular and got a lot of attention. But as i grew, my heroes changed so that now i can honestly say that anyone who does anything to help a child in this life is a hero to me.

In 1999, another award—and a special surprise—awaited Fred when he attended another huge celebration where he was inducted into the Hall of Fame. With Rogers himself still seated in front of the stage, the event's announcer called a very special guest in—Jeffrey Erlanger, who had been a guest on *Mister Roger's Neighborhood* in 1980. Erlanger met Rogers for an episode of the show in which he showed Rogers and his audience the wheelchair he had been in since becoming a quadriplegic. Only five years old, Jeffrey had received life-saving surgery to remove a cancerous tumor from his brain. Unable to walk afterward, he learned to use a wheelchair. Shocked and obviously delighted to see Jeffrey, Rogers stood immediately and climbed directly onto the stage to give his friend a hug.

Said Erlanger, after exchanging happy greetings: "When you tell people 'it's you I like,' we know that you really mean it. And tonight, I want to let you know on behalf of millions of children and grown-ups, it is you that I like."

Again, audience members struggled to hold in their tears while applauding enthusiastically. Once he collected himself—which in classic Mister Rogers fashion only took a moment—Fred told his fans: "Fame is a four-letter word, and…what ultimately matters is what we do with it."

Though it seemed America's favorite children's storyteller had received every formal acknowledgment there was to receive, there was one more prestigious award left. The Presidential Medal of Freedom serves as recognition of the outstanding service someone has made to their country, and as such, it is awarded by the President of the United States. In 2002, President George W. Bush presented Fred Rogers with that very award in the East Room of the White House on the 9th of July. Photos of the event show both Rogers and Bush grinning before the president affixed the medal around Fred's neck. Only half a year after the joyous ceremony, hundreds of mourners attended their favorite neighbor's funeral at Heinz Hall in Pittsburgh.

Forty-three honorary doctorate degrees were presented to Rogers over the course of his career, and for each one he received, he kept the ceremonial hood he wore when speaking to graduates at their commencement ceremonies. Friends of Fred turned many of those colorful hoods into two quilts, which are now kept at the Fred Rogers Center. One of these hoods, that of Roanoke College, was collected posthumously. Having agreed to receive an honorary degree and perform the commencement speech to graduates of Roanoke in 2003, Fred sadly died before the graduation took place. The graduation program for the 2003 commencement reads: "In recognition of Fred Rogers' dedication to children and his contributions to our society, the Board of Trustees of Roanoke College posthumously confers upon him the Honorary Degree of Doctor of Humane Letters."

Chapter Twenty-Two – Daniel Tiger's Neighborhood

After Fred's death, his company, Family Communications, was renamed after him: The Fred Rogers Company. The non-profit continued to organize and distribute *Mister Rogers' Neighborhood* after 2003, and in 2012, they started broadcasting *Daniel Tiger's Neighborhood* in Canada and the United States. Based on an animated character who was the son of Rogers' original Daniel Striped Tiger puppet, the show brought back wonderful memories and new stories all at once. After all, if Mister Rogers himself couldn't find the perfect host to replace himself in the Neighborhood, who better than a new generation of beloved tigers to help children learn about the important things in life?

Daniel Tiger and a cast of classic puppet offspring inhabit their own Neighborhood of Make-Believe as do their imaginary parents; only this time, everything is animated. The 4-year-old tiger cub mingles with O the Owl, Katerina Kittycat, Miss Elaina, and Prince Wednesday. To viewers of *Mister Rogers' Neighborhood*, that's the nephew of X the Owl, the daughter of Henrietta Pussycat, the daughter of Lady Elaine Fairchilde and Music Man Stan, and Prince Tuesday's little brother.

Though it all looks very similar to the original Neighborhood of Make-Believe, the world in which Daniel Tiger and his family live is actually located on Jungle Beach. Fortunately, all the other puppet members of Mister Rogers' Land of Make-Believe have also moved to Jungle Beach, bringing their homes with them. There's the castle of King Friday and Queen Sara, Grandpere's clock tower, the Museum-Go-Round, and a big tree for Katerina Kittycat and O the Owl.

The little tiger himself acts the part of the host perfectly, putting on his red cardigan and matching sneakers while singing a quick and cheery version of "Won't You Be My Neighbor?" A miniature trolley sits behind him, and when Daniel runs outside to catch the big version of Trolley, we see that he lives in a grass-roofed hut. Trolley takes him all around the Neighborhood of Make-Believe, past all the young characters who wave and smile as he goes by. Then, just as it was before, the host takes his audience through a seemingly normal day that will inevitably reveal an important part of the real world.

In one episode, it turns out that Mom Tiger wants to take Daniel to the doctor for a shot. He runs to his room and hides under a blanket before looking at the imaginary camera and asking, "Have you ever had a shot?" Mom Tiger explains that sometimes it helps to imagine something else when getting a shot so you don't notice the pain. To get her point across, she sings "Close Your Eyes and Think of Something Happy," and Daniel Tiger joins in while playing with his pretend doctor kit.

Even though Daniel Tiger's home is really just a part of Mister Rogers' own Land of Make-Believe, the tiger cub host still takes time out of his day to practice his own make-believe. The imaginary story grows out of a thought bubble in which Daniel becomes Super

Daniel, a brave tiger with the super-speed and flying abilities needed to help all his friends when trouble strikes. The make-believe segments are a feature of each 22-minute episode of *Daniel Tiger's Neighborhood*, as are what the producers call "strategy songs." Many of these songs are available in albums under the artist name "Daniel Tiger's Neighborhood."

The series was created by Kevin Morrison and Angela Santomero, the latter of whom also created the children's television hit *Blue's Clues*. Proudly televised by PBS, the network's website has games and videos based on *Daniel Tiger's Neighborhood* that children can watch and play or parents can use for family activities. There's even a character page that explains how each member of the new *Neighborhood* cast is related to a member of the original cast. Dad Tiger, the new incarnation of Daniel Striped Tiger, is kind of shy. He wears a blue zip-up cardigan and works in the clock factory. In his free time, Daniel Tiger Senior enjoys playing the trumpet and taking photographs.

In addition to Daniel Tiger's show, the Fred Roger's Company produces three other children's television shows: *Peg + Cat*, *Odd Squad*, and *Through the Woods*. According to the company's website, "Fred Rogers Productions inspires a lifetime of learning by creating quality children's media that models an enthusiasm for learning and earns the trust of parents and caregivers." Each program is meant to prepare preschool and young kids for school situations, particularly in terms of social interactions. Additional materials such as books and games are available online, and the programs themselves are purchasable on CD so families can choose their own viewing times—just as Mister Rogers hoped they would with VCR-recorded copies in the 1970s and onward.

In 2018, the creators of the Daniel Tiger show released *A Daniel Tiger Movie: Won't You Be Our Neighbor?* Through the adorable personal stories and imagination of Daniel Tiger and his friends, it looks like the kindly ways of Mister Rogers will live on in more than just reruns. And best of all, producers promise parents that the shows will continue to be full of loving references to the man who made all this possible: the irreplaceable Fred Rogers.

For all his diligence, concern, and determination to make the most of his time on earth, Fred Rogers will be remembered and loved by those whose hearts he touched and whose minds he helped to shape. As he often said, we are all pieced together from things our loved ones have done and said—and so, he will live on for generations to come.

Here's another book that you might be interested in

References

The Huffington Post. "What Would Mister Rogers Eat? Thanksgiving in the Neighborhood." 21 January 2015.

NPR. "Walking The Beat In Mr. Rogers' Neighborhood, Where A New Day Began Together." 11 March 2016.

Pittsburgh Post Gazette. "The Music of Mister Rogers." 19 February 2018.

Rogers, Fred. *The World According to Mister Rogers: Important Things to Remember.* 2003.

Rogers, Fred. "Senate Statement on PBS Funding." American Rhetoric, Online Speech Bank, 1 May 1969.

Carter, Alison. *USA Today.* "This Mr. Rogers story will probably make you cry." 23 May 2017.

People. "Fred Rogers Moves into a New Neighborhood—and So Does His Rebellious Son." 15 May 1978.

LA Times. "Fred Rogers' family keeps the legacy of 'Mister Rogers' Neighborhood' alive with a candid new documentary." 12 June 2018.

NPR. "It's a Beautiful 50th Birthday for 'Mister Rogers' Neighborhood.'" 19 February 2018.

ABC News. "Michael Keaton opens up about working for Fred Rogers." Retrieved from https://abcnews.go.com/GMA/video/michael-keaton-opens-up-about-working-with-fred-rogers-26187686.